Historic Landmarks of Old New York

Museyon Guides

New York

Library of Congress Cataloging-in-Publication Data

Title: Historic landmarks of old New York / edited by Museyon Guides.
Description: New York : Museyon Guides, [2017} | Series: Historic landmarks series.
Identifiers: ISBN: 978-1-940842-15-8 | LCCN: 2017933992
Subjects: LCSH: New York (N.Y.)--Guidebooks. | New York (N.Y.)--Pictorial works. | Manhattan (New York, N.Y.)--Guidebooks. | Manhattan (New York, N.Y.)--Pictorial works. | Neighborhoods--New York (State)--New York--Guidebooks. | Historic sites--New York (State)--New York--Guidebooks. | Historic sites--New York (State)--New York--Pictorial works. | Historic buildings--New York (State)--New York--Guidebooks. | Historic buildings--New York (State)--New York--Pictorial works. | New York (N.Y.)--History--Miscellanea. | New York (N.Y.)--Biography--Miscellanea. | LCGFT: Guidebooks. | BISAC: TRAVEL / United States / Northeast / Middle Atlantic (NJ, NY, PA)
Classification: LCC: F128.37 .H57 2017 | DDC: 974.7/1--dc23

Published in the United States by:
Museyon Inc.
1177 Avenue of the Americas, 5th Floor
New York, NY 10036

Museyon is a registered trademark.
Visit us online at www.museyon.com

ISBN 978-1-940842-15-8

0714120

Printed in China

> *"There is something in the New York air that makes sleep useless."*

> *—Simone de Beauvoir*

Restless, industrious, on the make and on the move, Manhattan, the heart of New York, is a fascinating place. But the energy, fast pace and modernity of the city today often mask its deep-rooted and deeply revered past. Luckily, many of the places where the visionaries, risk-takers, dreamers and schemers, who built—and continue to build—New York and the United States, survive. However transformed and redefined they have become over the years, decades and centuries, these structures, made of brick and mortar, marble and limestone, steel and glass—and not to forget: blood, sweat and tears—all bear witness to the city's richness, power and, above all, importance.

This guidebook explores ninety-nine of these historically significant landmarks. Vintage photographs that attest to the city's aesthetic beauty and gritty humanity accompany the text, while quirky, often outrageous, celebrity quotes enliven the history lesson. Sooner or later, anyone who is anyone makes a pilgrimage to "the city that never sleeps," and everyone has an opinion. New York is a city about which it is impossible to be indifferent.

So, get inspired by the same air that Simone de Beauvoir once breathed and never need sleep again—when you're in New York!

Historic Landmarks of Old New York

Table of Contents

Old New York Anecdotes

New York Harbor and Downtown/ Financial District

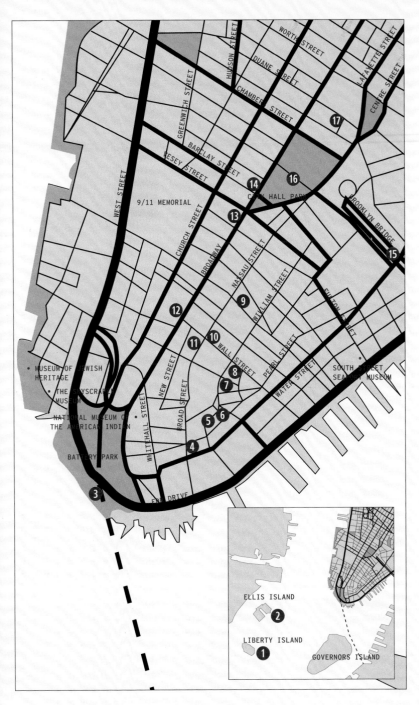

MUSEUM OF JEWISH
HERITAGE

THE SKYSCRAPER
MUSEUM

NATIONAL MUSEUM OF
THE AMERICAN INDIAN

BATTERY PARK

9/11 MEMORIAL

WEST STREET

GREENWICH STREET

HUDSON STREET

DUANE STREET

WORTH STREET

CHAMBERS STREET

BARCLAY STREET

VESEY STREET

CHURCH STREET

BROADWAY

NASSAU STREET

WILLIAM STREET

LAFAYETTE STREET

CENTRE STREET

CITY HALL PARK

BROOKLYN BRIDGE

WALL STREET

PEARL STREET

FULTON STREET

WATER STREET

SOUTH STREET
SEAPORT MUSEUM

NEW STREET

BROAD STREET

WHITEHALL STREET

FDR DRIVE

17

16

14

13

15

12

9

11 **10**

8

7

6

5

4

3

ELLIS ISLAND

2

LIBERTY ISLAND

1

GOVERNORS ISLAND

*Make your mark in New York
and you are a made man.*

—*Mark Twain*

{ The Statue of Liberty }

A symbol of America's freedom in general and New York City's opportunity in particular, The Statue of Liberty's home is actually part of New Jersey.

Lady Liberty, with her flowing gown and impenetrable gaze, was conceived and designed by Frédéric-Auguste Bartholdi after being inspired by the words of French law professor and politician Édouard René de Laboulaye. At a dinner party in 1865, Laboulaye commented that any monument raised to American independence would be a joint venture of both countries. Work began on the statue in 1870; the French financed the figure and America provided the pedestal.

Immigrant family looking at the Statue of Liberty from Ellis Island

Bartholdi completed the head and torch-bearing arm before funding was raised for the rest of the body. The arm and torch were put on display in Madison Square Park from 1876 to 1882, while the head and crown were exhibited at the 1878 Paris World Fair. The full statue was completed and erected in 1886 and was marked by New York's first ticker-tape parade.

Closed for years post-September 11 and extensively repaired in 2011, the statue is today a magnet for millions of visitors who flock to Liberty Island to see New York City's most recognizable attraction—even if it is a New Jersey gem.

Who Discovered New York?

Although Henry Hudson is commonly known as the man who discovered New York, Giovanni da Verrazzano beat him to the punch.

The Italian navigator secured a deal with King Francis I to explore the New World on behalf of France. He began his voyage on January 17, 1524, aboard the Delfina, with a mission to expand France's empire and find passages to the Pacific Ocean and Asia. Sailing along the territory's northern coastline, he also hoped to discover waterways to North America's west coast. He reached New York Bay that April and later pushed north to Martha's Vineyard, with a final stop in Rhode Island before heading home.

Also looking for a passage to Asia, Englishman Henry Hudson made a similar journey for the Dutch in 1609. Exploring more of the area than his predecessor, and eventually reaching today's Albany, his findings led to Dutch colonization of New Amsterdam and a more memorable place in history.

As for Verrazzano, he did return to the New World twice. Unfortunately, the third time wasn't a charm. While exploring the Lesser Antilles, he was ambushed and eaten by cannibals. The Verrazzano-Narrows bridge, connecting Brooklyn to Staten Island, is named in his honor.

Giovanni da Verrazzano (left) and Henry Hudson

Everywhere immigrants have enriched and strengthened the fabric of American life.

—*John F. Kennedy*

{ Ellis Island }

Before 1890, individual states had to monitor foreign entry into the country. With the mass migration throughout the late 19th century, the federal government stepped in and set up a central immigration station on Ellis Island in the upper New York Bay, just off the New Jersey coast.

Irish teenager Annie Moore was the first immigrant processed at Ellis Island, the new national gateway to freedom, which opened in 1892. Over the next 62 years, more than 12 million people would follow in her footsteps. The station's main building is now a national museum, recounting its history through exhibitions and tours.

Go down to the North River and the benches that run along the west side of Battery Park City. Watch the tides or the blocks of ice in winter; they have existed since the time when the island was empty of man.

—Pete Hamill

{ Castle Clinton }

In the early 1800s, forts were built throughout New York City to protect the nation's first capital from invasion. Castle Clinton, constructed in 1808, was built on a manmade island off Manhattan's west coast. Later, the water was filled in to create an extension of the city.

Before Ellis Island was built, Castle Clinton was the Emigrant Landing Depot from 1855 to 1890. It was the New York City Aquarium from 1896 to 1941 until the attraction moved to Coney Island. Today, it's a visitor center, exhibition space and ticketing office for cruises to the Statue of Liberty and Ellis Island.

With a heart full of love and gratitude, I now take leave of you. I most devoutly wish that your latter days may be as prosperous and happy as your former ones have been glorious and honorable.

—George Washington

{ Fraunces Tavern }

The first building to sit on the corner of Pearl and Broad streets was constructed in 1671 as a home for New York Mayor Stephanus Van Cortlandt and remained in his family for several generations until tavern keeper Samuel Fraunces bought it in 1762.

During its first decade as a tavern, the popular watering hole was a hotbed for pre-American Revolutionary War activity. A secret society of patriots, known as the Sons of Liberty, powwowed there, discussing colonists' rights and condemning British rule.

George Washington bids farewell to his officers at Fraunces Tavern, 1783

Activity at the tavern didn't slow down during the war either. For example, a British ship hurled a cannonball through the roof. After the war, when New York City became the nation's first capital, the building housed several governmental offices, including the departments of Foreign Affairs, War and Finance.

Today, the museum space on the second and third floors features historic documents, American Revolution-era art and artifacts, and period rooms. Of particular interest is the Long Room, where George Washington said farewell to his officers at the end of the war.

The street-level restaurant features a menu of morsels that Washington and company might have enjoyed during their day, with ciders and whiskeys to wash down the steaks, chops and oysters.

Peter Minuit's Exchange of Manhattan, 1626

"The Purchase of Manhattan Island by Peter Minuit in 1626," William T. Ranney, c. 1855

What the Dutch West India Company paid for Manhattan Island takes the term "low-balling" to a whole new level.

The trading company, formed in 1621, held a monopoly on colonization in the Americas. In 1625, it sent Peter Minuit, a former church deacon and diamond cutter, to protect its interests in the New World, establishing solid trading relationships with Indian tribes up and down the Hudson and Delaware rivers.

He returned in May the following year, this time with a promotion and a loftier goal. As New Netherland's third director, he was tasked with purchasing Manhattan from the island's natives.

Some might call Minuit a shrewd salesman, while others believe the Lenape didn't understand the concept of land ownership and thought they were simply ensuring colonists' safety. Either way, Minuit got the land for a steal, paying 60 guilders worth of beads, cloth and ornaments for ownership rights.

The deal consolidated the scattered settlements and furthered development of Fort Amsterdam on the southern tip of Manhattan. The agreement was more than likely made in that area, specifically where the Peter Minuit Plaza at the Staten Island Ferry Terminal now stands. A boulder in Inwood Hill Park at the northern tip also marks the historic event.

I go to Paris, I go to London, I go to Rome, and I always say, 'There's no place like New York.' It's the most exciting city in the world now. That's the way it is. That's it.

—Robert De Niro

{ Stone Street Historic District }

Comprised of 15 historic buildings along the winding, narrow pathways of Pearl, South William and Stone streets, as well as Hanover Square, Coenties Alley and Mill Lane, the area known as the Stone Street Historic District dates back to the 17th century. When New York was still New Amsterdam, Dutch colonists set up clusters of mercantile shops here. Although the Great Fire of 1835 razed all of the area's original structures, residents quickly rebuilt, filling the space with storefronts for merchants and importers.

The earlier businesses are long gone, but many historic structures now house restaurants and bars.

If London is a watercolor, New York is an oil painting.
—*Peter Shaffer*

{ India House }

Richard F. Carman built the Renaissance palazzo-style commercial building at 1 Hanover Square, known as India House, in 1851. Hanover Bank was the first owner; later, the New York Cotton Exchange (founded in 1870) occupied the space. It became a private club in 1914, a gathering spot for leaders in commerce. The building houses a collection of Chinese art objects, model ships and maritime paintings.

Captain Kidd and New York

Scotsman William Kidd was a successful privateer when he settled in New York. He lived with his socialite wife, Sarah Oort, and their two daughters at 119 Pearl Street.

He set sail in September 1696 on behalf of the Crown to rid the Eastern Seaboard of French ships and pirates. He was scheduled to return from his travels in March.

Although the journey was marred by misfortune, in February 1698, Kidd spotted the Quedagh Merchant— teeming with gold, silver, jewels, sugar, silk and guns— off the Indian coast. The Armenian merchant ship was owned by Indians, crewed by Moors, had Persian cargo and was captained by an Englishman. The ship held a French pass, so Kidd considered his conquest of it legitimate.

Kidd finally returned to New York in 1699, and was promptly arrested for piracy and murder. He left his ship in the hands of his crew but wouldn't reveal the location of his treasure. It was later learned that his crew had sold off the loot and set fire to the plundered ship. Kidd was put on trial in London and executed in 1701.

In 2007, the Quedagh Merchant's remains were discovered off the coast of Catalina Island, Dominican Republic. The treasure has yet to be unearthed.

"Captain Kidd in New York Harbor," Jean Leon Gerome Ferris, c. 1920

New York is the only real city-city.

—*Truman Capote*

{ 20 Exchange Place }

Opened in 1931 as the Wall Street headquarters for the
City Bank Farmers Trust Company—the earliest iteration
of today's CitiBank—the 57-floor tower is an Art Deco
classic, with a mixed-material facade of steel, stone, granite
and limestone. Elaborate nickel-silver doors with carvings
by British sculptor David Evans still grace the lobby, while
commercial spaces above are now luxury residences.

It is not down in any map; true places never are.
—*Herman Melville*

{ 55 Wall Street—Merchant Exchange }

The 1841 Greek Revival building has had many occupants, including the United States Custom House, where writer Herman Melville was employed. Melville penned "Moby Dick" while working there.

The massive ground floor, remodeled in the early 20th century to resemble the Roman Pantheon, now serves as an event space for upscale restaurant chain Cipriani.

I believe that banking institutions are more dangerous to our liberties than standing enemies.

—*Thomas Jefferson*

{ Federal Reserve Building }

If you think the Federal Reserve building looks like an impenetrable stone fortress designed to guard the world's riches, you are correct. The block-long Financial District building protects a sizable piggy bank. More than 6,000 tons of gold owned by foreign governments, central banks and international organizations are secured in a vault buried 80 feet below street level. Guided tours are available.

New York is a different country. Maybe it ought to have a separate government. Everybody thinks differently, they just don't know what the hell the rest of the United States is.

—Henry Ford

{ Federal Hall }

There is a common misconception surrounding the history of Federal Hall in Lower Manhattan, that it is the building in which George Washington was inaugurated as the nation's first president. While it is true that the building in which he was inaugurated once stood in the same location as the current Federal Hall, the Greek Revival-style building that now stands on Wall Street was built 139 years after the one in which Washington took his famous oath.

The original Federal Hall was built in 1703 and was used as New York's city hall. In those early years, the building held pinnacle moments in American history, such as the trial of

Old City Hall in 17

printer John Peter Zenger, whose acquittal on the charge of libel was a precedent-setting case for freedom of the press. In 1765, the Stamp Act Congress met there to protest "taxation without representation."

In 1788, the building was renamed Federal Hall and New York became the first capital of the United States. It is here that the Bill of Rights was passed. In 1789, Federal Hall was used as the site of the swearing in of Washington.

The original building was torn down in 1812, and a temporary, small brick building was constructed to serve as the U.S. Customs House. The building we see today was built in 1842.

George Washington and New York

On August 27, 1776, General Washington's Continental Army was heavily outnumbered by General Howe's British troops, who attacked the western end of Long Island in present-day Brooklyn. On August 29, the American commander had little choice but to send his men across the East River to Manhattan Island in the middle of the night. According to witnesses, Washington was the last to make the crossing.

The Battle of Long Island was one of many defeats patriots suffered before the war was over. However, the Continental Army never gave up its stronghold in the countryside, and on November 25, 1783, British troops left Manhattan, marking the end of the Revolutionary War.

Washington returned to the city in triumph, marching from his northern headquarters at Fort Washington, across the Harlem River and down to The Battery at the foot of Broadway. A week later, he formally said farewell to his troops during a festive banquet at Fraunces Tavern.

Washington next returned to Manhattan on April 30, 1789, for his inauguration as the nation's first president. Although the original Federal Hall building no longer stands, a statue of Washington rests in front of the current Federal Hall to mark the approximate place where he was sworn in.

A sign depicting the retreat over the East River at Fulton Ferry Landing in Brooklyn Bridge Park

Wall Street is the only place that people ride to in a Rolls-Royce to get advice from those who take the subway.

—Warren Buffett

{ New York Stock Exchange }

Long associated with the financial highs and lows of the world's leading corporations, architect George B. Post's Georgian marble structure opened for business in 1903. Although tours of the interior are no longer given, visitors to Lower Manhattan can take photos of the imposing exterior. The fortresslike facade features an expansive classical portico, fluted Corinthian columns and a triangular pediment containing sculptor John Quincy Adams Ward's grouping, "Integrity Protecting the Works of Man." Also of interest is the building's Wall Street side, which still bears marks from a 1920 bombing for which the perpetrators were never caught.

It is my desire to receive the communion at your hands. I hope you will not conceive there is any impropriety in my request.

—Alexander Hamilton

{ Trinity Church }

Now dwarfed by dozens of 20th- and 21st-century skyscrapers that dot Lower Manhattan's landscape, the third and current Trinity Church was the tallest building in the nation when it was erected in 1846. City dwellers could see its towering Gothic Revival spire from afar.

Resting on the same site as its predecessors, the structure has hosted many dignitaries throughout its history, including Queen Elizabeth II, who visited in 1976. Although the church broke its ties with England and the monarch after the Revolutionary War, officials presented the church's former landlord with a special gift. As a humorous nod to the church's

Queen Elizabeth II visited Trinity Church in 1976

past, the queen was given 279 peppercorns as back rent, per King William III's original 1697 agreement requiring an annual rent payment of one peppercorn to the crown.

While exploring the cavernous space, make sure to snap Instagram-worthy pictures of Richard Morris Hunt's series of bronze doors, featuring a visual history of New York, the church and biblical events; marvel at the stained-glass windows; read historic documents in the museum, including the original charter; listen to free choral concerts; and enjoy a leisurely stroll through the cemetery, where Alexander Hamilton, inventor Robert Fulton and other important figures are interred.

The Great Negro Plot, 1741

Racial tensions led to the witch-hunt-like event that occurred in New York in 1741.

On February 28, someone broke into Robert Hogg's home at the corner of Broad and South William streets. The stolen goods, including a few linens, were found in the possession of John Hughson, a saloon owner who catered to slaves and was known for embracing deviant behavior in his tavern. The event was soon followed by a series of mysterious arson attacks, beginning with a fire at Fort George.

The fire investigator was eager to link the burglary and fires and questioned Hughson's servant, Mary Burton. Officials bribed and threatened the young girl, leading her to concoct a story that would bring race relations to one of the lowest points in the city's history.

Burton told the authorities that slaves were planning to burn down the city, kill all the white residents, except for Hughson, and crown the saloon owner as "King of New York." Her lie enraged white colonists, who, in retaliation, executed 31 African Americans (many met their demise while burning at the stake) as well as Hughson and his wife. An additional 154 people were imprisoned, while 71 were exiled to the West Indies.

St. Paul's Chapel stands—without so much as a broken window. Little miracle.

—Rudy Giuliani

{ St. Paul's Chapel }

Completed in 1766, St. Paul's Chapel is the oldest surviving church building on Manhattan Island. It was almost destroyed in the Great Fire of 1776—an inferno that wiped out nearly 1,000 buildings—and that wouldn't be the last time it would dodge destruction.

Before the Revolutionary War, Founding Father Alexander Hamilton practiced militia drills in the courtyard. When the new nation won its freedom, George Washington prayed in the chapel on April 30, 1789, following his inauguration as the first president of the United States at nearby Federal Hall. Washington would return often over the next two years (when

New York City was the nation's capital); an oil painting of the Great Seal of the United States hangs above his pew.

More than two centuries later, volunteers sifting through wreckage from the September 11, 2001, World Trade Center terrorist attacks would rest in St. Paul's during breaks—even the president's pew served as a bed for weary relief workers. Although located fewer than 100 yards from the Twin Towers, the chapel was unharmed during the attacks, which earned it the nickname "The Little Chapel That Stood." Most thank a sturdy sycamore tree for taking the force of the impact.

P.T. Barnum's Circus and Museum

Barnum's American Museum on Broadway and Ann Street, 1853

Before dazzling audiences with his world-renowned circus, P.T. Barnum owned a museum on Broadway and Ann Street in Lower Manhattan. Barnum's American Museum housed a freak show, magicians, jugglers, animals, wax figures and the country's first aquarium. It was also home base for his traveling acts, including General Tom Thumb.

The building, the former Scudder's American Museum, was renovated by Barnum to be as magnificent as the exhibits inside. He added an attention-grabbing lighthouse lamp, roof flags and giant paintings of animals on the facade. Visitors took in bird's-eye views from the roof garden, while thrill-seekers enjoyed expansive vistas on hot-air balloon rides.

More than 38 million people visited the museum during its reign as the city's most popular attraction. The fun ended in 1865 when the museum, which opened in 1841, burned to the ground. Barnum tried to revive the institution in another location but that also succumbed to fire.

His circus career began in the 1870s, when he established P. T. Barnum's Grand Traveling Museum, Menagerie, Caravan & Hippodrome. The following decade, he joined forces with James Bailey to create Barnum & Bailey Circus. The three-ring spectacle featured many attractions from his former museum, with the addition of Jumbo the Elephant.

We still have the Chrysler Building and the Empire State Building and the Woolworth Building, but it just seems like part of the nature of New York, that it's always shifting.

—Richard Hell

{ The Woolworth Building }

F.W. Woolworth's "Cathedral of Commerce" was the tallest building in the world when completed in 1913. On opening day, President Woodrow Wilson pressed a button in the White House to illuminate the Beaux Arts building's ornate, mosaic-filled interior and Gothic facade. In its heyday, the structure housed offices, a shopping center, health club, restaurant and social club. Later, the landmark was headquarters for payroll for the Manhattan Project—the World War II-era research and development project that produced the first nuclear weapons. Although the skyscraper is now closed to the public, tours of its lobby reveal its many architectural splendors.

*When Charles first saw our child Mary,
he said all the proper things for a new
father. He looked upon the poor little
red thing and blurted, 'She's more
beautiful than the Brooklyn Bridge.'*

—Helen Hayes

{ Brooklyn Bridge }

Before tunnels and highways linked the city's five boroughs, 19th-century nine-to-fivers would take the ferry across the East River from Brooklyn to Manhattan. All that changed on May 24, 1883, the day the Brooklyn Bridge opened. With its weblike network of steel cables, imposing granite beams and Gothic towers, New York City's iconic suspension bridge—more than 13 years in the making—was the longest of its kind at the time.

Throughout its history, thrill-seekers have eagerly tested their courage and the structure's durability. Circus owner P.T. Barnum marched 21 elephants over it, while swimming

Frank Sinatra, Jules Munshin and Gene Kelly on the Brooklyn Bridge from the film "On the Town," 1949

instructor Robert E. Odlum was the first of many to dive from the structure into the choppy waters below. Daredevils still try to snag headlines by scaling the cables.

A stroll on the bridge's pedestrian promenade is an adventurous way to see the Brooklyn and Manhattan cityscapes. The round-trip is two miles, so wear comfortable shoes and bring along a bottle of water. If you cross the bridge with your sweetheart, also bring along a padlock: It's a romantic tradition. Couples hang locks bearing their names on the bridge to symbolize eternal love, and then throw the keys into the river to represent everlasting romance.

Robert Fulton and New York Ferries

In 1787, Robert Fulton traveled to London to study portraiture painting. He found little success as an artist, but what he did discover was an interest in the steam engine and how to use it on the water—from creating canals for inland water transportation to developing submarines for naval warfare.

During his time in Europe, he also met Robert R. Livingston, U.S. Minister to France and the exclusive rights holder to steam navigation on the Hudson River. Fulton built a small steamboat and tested it on the Seine. Impressed, Livingston told him to make a larger version for commercial use on New York waterways.

In August 1807, Fulton's 150-foot-long North River Steamboat made her trial

Robert Fulton's North River Steamboat, later known as the Clermont

run, a 150-mile voyage from New York City to Albany. With a single-cylinder condensing steam engine powered by oak and pine fuel, the steamboat glided up the river with ease, completing the journey in 32 hours. It took sailing sloops four days by comparison. Soon, Fulton's invention was operating regular service, with several stops along the river. His steamship ferry route revolutionized commutes from Manhattan to Brooklyn, crossing the East River in 12 minutes. The Fulton streets in Brooklyn and Manhattan were drop-off and pick-up points.

Stop them damn pictures!
I don't care what the papers write
about me. My constituents can't read.
But, damn it, they can see the pictures!

—*"Boss" Tweed*

{ New York City Hall }

Featuring an ornate, alabaster-hued facade—complete with arched windows, Ionic and Corinthian columns and pillars, and a cupola topped with a statue of Justice—New York's current City Hall, its third, is the oldest in the nation still to retain its civic purpose.

Officially opened in 1812, the Federal-style, three-tiered building in Lower Manhattan has been the setting of many poignant moments in United States history. After his assassination, President Abraham Lincoln's body lay in state in the Georgian rotunda; two decades later, the body of President Ulysses S. Grant was also on view in the rotunda.

City Hall Station

Modern-day visitors can see an extensive collection of portraiture and President George Washington's desk in the Governor's Room. The grounds surrounding City Hall are also worth a gander. The sprawling green space boasts monuments and temporary installations. If you want to go off the beaten path, head to the old City Hall subway station exit near the west side of the park. From there, you can peer down into the turn-of-the-last-century terminal's skylights embedded in the nearby concrete. Only in operation from 1904 to 1945, the terminal's vibrant green-and-beige Guastavino tiles; vaulted, cathedral-like ceiling; and chandeliers look as they did when first installed.

Allyson Schettino
Associate Director of School Programs
New-York Historical Society

One hundred years before Rosa Parks refused to move to the back of the bus, New Yorker Elizabeth Jennings led the fight to desegregate the New York City trolley system. In 1854, Jennings, an African-American school teacher and church organist, was running late to Sunday mass at the First Colored American Congregational Church and hailed a "whites only trolley" at the corner of Pearl and Chatham (now Park Row) streets. When the conductor asked her to get off and wait for a car for "her people," Jennings refused, a fight broke out, and she was dragged from the car by the conductor and a policeman. Furious, Jennings wrote an account of the incident that was circulated to her church community and subsequently published in the New York Tribune. With the backing of her father and other African American leaders, Jennings hired young lawyer and future president Chester A. Arthur and sued the trolley company. She won her case, and the trolley company was forced to desegregate its cars. Inspired by her victory, the Legal Rights Association filed more successful suits against other trolley companies, effectively ending the segregation of public transit in New York.

New-York Historical Society: 170 Central Park West, New York

American slavery was not a Sergio Leone Spaghetti Western. It was a holocaust. My ancestors are slaves. Stolen from Africa. I will honor them.

—Spike Lee

{ African Burial Ground }

New buildings are constantly popping up in the city. In 1991, construction for a federal office building in downtown's Civic Center unearthed more than bedrock. Workers found skeletal remains on what archaeologists would later discover was a 6.6-acre burial ground, used from the 1690s until 1794 for free and enslaved Africans, and located just outside the New Amsterdam settlement.

During excavation, the remains of 419 men, women and children were unearthed, as well as wooden grave markers, in the largest bio-archaeological site of its kind. The remains were reinterred there in 2003. It's now a National Monument.

Lower East Side, SoHo, Washington Square

If you live in New York, even if you're Catholic, you're Jewish.

—Lenny Bruce

{ Eldridge Street Synagogue }

Built by Peter and Francis William Herter in 1887, Eldridge Street Synagogue is one of the first synagogues built by Eastern European Jews in the country. The Moorish Revival building's interior includes 70-foot-high vaulted ceilings and magnificent stained-glass windows.

A popular temple for the city's Jewish population, the synagogue expanded its mission to aid the poor and help make arrangements for the sick and dying. Membership dwindled after the 1920s, and the building fell into disrepair. In 1986, the Eldridge Street Project, a nonprofit, was created to restore the historic space. In 2007, it reopened as the Museum at Eldridge Street.

Everybody ought to have a Lower East Side in their life.

—Irving Berlin

{ Tenement Museum }

There's no denying modern-day New Yorkers are used to cramped living conditions, but accommodations were even more confined for the city's 19th-century newcomers. Dating back as early as the 1820s, the Lower East Side was filled with thousands of tenements—modest buildings divided into tiny apartments, serving as cheap housing and commercial space for the city's immigrant families. Today, the unassuming structure at 97 Orchard Street is one of the city's last remaining tenements.

Opened by German immigrant Lukas Glockner in 1863, the building housed an estimated 7,000 people before shuttering its doors in 1935. Essentially

Sunday morning at Orchard and Rivington Streets, c. 1915

a place for city laborers to rest their weary heads at night, the building offered the bare minimum. Inhabitants had to rely on coal-burning stoves for heat, while indoor toilets weren't added until after 1901 and electric light until 1924.

After years of disuse, the building reopened as a museum in 1992. Today, through guided tours, visitors can see six restored apartments, including the German-Jewish Gumpertz and Italian-Catholic Baldizzi family homes, learn more about immigrant life (both past and present) and explore the rich history of the surrounding Lower East Side neighborhood via walking tours. The museum also operates a visitor center and exhibition space at 103 Orchard Street.

Jacob Riis, "How the Other Half Lives"

"Five Cents a Spot, Unauthorized Immigrant Lodgings in a Bayard Street Tenement" from "How the Other Half Lives"

While wealthy and middle-class New Yorkers enjoyed comfortable conditions in the rest of the city, many had no idea how bad life was for poor immigrants on the Lower East Side. Jacob Riis' pictorial essay opened their eyes (and hearts) to life in the slums of turn-of-the-last-century New York.

Riis, born in Denmark, moved to New York in 1870 and lived in the densely populated area. He went on to become a successful crime reporter and wrote about his former home. Armed with a camera, he later gave visual proof of the deplorable conditions—from shoeless children huddling together for warmth on dirty street corners or manning machinery in sweatshops to robbers loitering on Mulberry Bend (the most crime-infested area in the city) while somber men and women slept in crowded, dilapidated tenements.

Riis, also a devout Christian, showed his findings in lecture halls, calling for audiences to abandon their complacency. Soon, his work was immortalized in magazine articles that reached the rest of the nation. In 1890, the series was compiled into a book, "How the Other Half Lives: Studies Among the Tenements of New York." His opus led to legislative reform on tenement safety, child labor laws and more.

It is ridiculous to set a detective story in New York City. New York City is itself a detective story.

—*Agatha Christie*

{ The Police Building }

Boasting the aesthetic appeal of a Parisian palace, with eye-catching domes, ornate pediments and intricate carvings, it's easy to imagine this 1909 Edwardian Baroque-style gem as the luxury condominium building it is today. But during its 64-year tenure as headquarters of the New York Police Department, it served as the containment facility for gangsters like Al Capone, John Dillinger and other members of the city's underbelly, who were processed, booked and interrogated here.

Across the street is Onieals Soho, a restaurant and bar. Rumor has it an underground tunnel connected the two buildings, letting Prohibition-era cops enjoy illegal libations undetected.

There is no place like it, no place with an atom of its glory, pride, and exultancy. It lays its hand upon a man's bowels; he grows drunk with ecstasy; he grows young and full of glory, he feels that he can never die.

—*Walt Whitman*

{ The Ear Inn }

James Brown, an African aide to George Washington during the Revolutionary War, built his Federal-style home in 1770 in what is today's SoHo. Back then, it was just five feet from the Hudson River.

By 1817, the area was teeming with ports, and the house turned into a brewery to serve thirsty sailors. By century's end, the tavern also included a restaurant and dining room.

Lauded as NYC's oldest bar, the establishment only got an official name in the 1970s. Owners cleverly masked parts of the "B" in the illuminated "BAR" sign to form "EAR"—avoiding the Landmark Commission's tedious review of new signage.

*Once you have lived in New York and it
has become your home, no place else is
good enough.”*

—John Steinbeck

{ St. Luke's Place }

While walking down Seventh Avenue South, make a right on Leroy Street. There's a bend in the road called St. Luke's Place, a tranquil stretch teeming with charming rowhouses built between 1852 and 1853.

In 1851, Trinity Church sold its land across from St. John's cemetery (now James J. Walker Park) for housing. Soon 15 three-story rowhouses occupied the lot. By the early 20th century, artists and authors had moved in, notably novelist Theodore Dreiser who penned "An American Tragedy" in No. 16. If the doorway at No. 10 looks familiar, it was the opening shot in "The Cosby Show."

Whenever spring comes to New York I can't stand the suggestions of the land that come blowing over the river from New Jersey and I've got to go.
So I went.

—Jack Kerouac

{ Judson Memorial Church }

Known as a space for groundbreaking exhibitions and avant-garde dance recitals, Judson Memorial Church is actually a house of worship and has been since its inception.

Baptist minister Edward Judson set up his Stanford White-designed, West Village temple in the late 1890s to serve downtown's Protestant population. Soon, it offered community outreach programs as well as religious ministries. Since the 1950s, the church has hosted exhibitions by the likes of Robert Rauschenberg and Yoko Ono, and dance productions by John Cage and Merce Cunningham.

Never deviating from its mission, Judson Memorial still assists a diverse congregation, community and roster of artists.

New York was a city where you could be frozen to death in the midst of a busy street and nobody would notice.

—Bob Dylan

{ Washington Square Park }

With its manicured lawns and meandering pathways, the recreation hub and forum for New York University students, tourists and everyone in between is Greenwich Village's most popular green space. However, in the past, the 9.75-acre plot served as farmland for freed slaves, a potter's field and a parade ground for the city's volunteer militia. An early version of today's park took shape in 1870.

In 1911, locals gathered there to mourn the 146 garment workers who died in the Triangle Shirtwaist Factory fire a block away (the building still stands at

23-29 Washington Place). The city's worst industrial disaster led to laws requiring better safety conditions for workers.

By the mid-20th century, the neighborhood was full of artists, and Washington Square Park was their stage. A then-unknown Jackson Pollock sold his paintings for rent money at the park's Outdoor Art Exhibition in the 1930s (an event that still exists today), while the 1960s saw Bob Dylan rock out by the fountain and Allen Ginsburg recite poetry on the lawn.

On any given day, you can watch live theater productions, listen to indie musicians, join demonstrations, play chess, picnic or simply sit near Stanford White's marble Washington Arch and people-watch.

Washington Square: Hangman's Elm and Rose Butler

The English elm at Waverly Place and MacDougal Street on Washington Square Park's northwest corner holds the distinction of being the oldest tree in Manhattan.

As legend has it, traitors were hanged from its branches during the Revolutionary War. When the area was a potter's field, prisoners from nearby Newgate State Prison, on Christopher and 10th streets, were hanged from its gallows. Some believe others also met their fates at the 110-foot tree, nicknamed Hangman's Elm.

The last-known person to be publicly executed by hanging from the potter's field gallows was Rose Butler. In 1818, the 19-year-old slave was accused of setting fire to her master's kitchen and

Hangman's Elm in Washington Square Park

tying a string on the door to prevent escape. No one was hurt, and only a few steps were burned.

When Butler was arrested, she claimed two men helped her set the fire, but they were never caught.

Her case raised questions as to whether arson was a capital or common law offense. Eventually, the case was sent to the Supreme Court, which deemed her crime a capital offense. Butler was hanged from the gallows on July 9, 1819.

Moved into the new studio which abounds in suggestion and inspiration.

—Gertrude Vanderbilt Whitney

{ MacDougal Alley }

Sculptor, collector and wealthy patron of the arts Gertrude Vanderbilt Whitney made a lasting impact on this charming lane, where artists transformed abandoned stables into studios. Her workshop in a former hayloft there served as the first Whitney Museum of American Art in 1931. The historic space is regularly open for tours; otherwise, the alley is usually closed to the public.

Strange now to think of you, gone without corsets & eyes, while I walk on the sunny pavement of Greenwich Village.—Allen Ginsberg

{ Washington Mews }

Built in 1883 to house stables for townhouses on Washington Square North and Eighth Street, Washington Mews is one of only a handful of alleys of its kind that still exist in the city. Most of the former stables on the Belgian-block-paved path are now two-story buildings occupied by New York University facilities, such as Deutsches Haus, which hosts an annual exhibition of Berlin-based students' artwork.

Greenwich Village/West Village

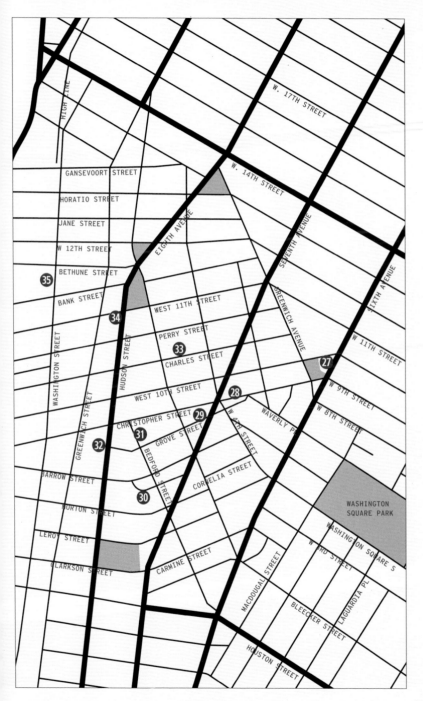

*On the contrary, your Honor, I
was doin' my best to conceal it.*

—Mae West

{ Jefferson Market Courthouse }

Greenwich Village's Frederick Clark Withers and
Calvert Vaux-designed courthouse, built between
1875 and 1877, boasts an impressive Victorian
Gothic-style facade. Nineteenth-century architects
voted it one of the 10 most beautiful buildings in
America. Part of a three-building complex (including
market housing and a jail, where Mae West spent the
night, booked on obscenity charges for her Broadway
hit "Sex"), the courthouse was shut down in 1945.

It has been a New York Public Library since
1967: The second-floor Adult Reading Room was
the civil court, the first-floor Children's Room the
police court, and the basement Reference Room the
prisoner holding area.

Most of my friends in New York are single women or gay men.

—Sarah Jessica Parker

{ Stonewall Inn }

By the 1960s, Greenwich Village had blossomed into a gay community. Homosexuality was legal in New York, but serving alcohol to gay customers was not. Hence, many gay bars operated without liquor licenses, making them prime targets for police and State Liquor Authority raids.

Stonewall Inn on Christopher Street—two carriage houses fused together in the 1930s—was a popular neighborhood hangout and subject to many of these attacks. During the wee hours of June 28, 1969, eight officers gathered for a routine raid of the bar, which not only served booze but also let gays dance together (another illegal act). However, the

Stonewall Inn raid c
June 28, 1969

200 patrons inside refused to cooperate this time. Gay New Yorkers had had enough.

When an officer hit a lesbian over the head with a billy club and hurled her into a paddy wagon, the hundreds of onlookers outside the bar took action, throwing bottles and bricks at the vehicle and the building, where outnumbered police waited for help. The Gay Rights movement had begun.

Today, the site of the 1969 Stonewall Uprising—including the bar, Christopher Park and the surrounding streets— is a National Historic Landmark, the first U.S. National Monument dedicated to LGBTQ civil rights.

Who Is Christopher of Christopher Street?

Many downtown roads are named after former landowners, including Christopher Street, the oldest path in the West Village.

In the early days of Old New York, the street ran along the south boundary of Admiral Sir Peter Warren's estate. For a short time, it was dubbed Skinner Road after Warren's son-in-law, Colonel William Skinner. In 1799, the land passed to Richard Amos, a trustee of the Warren estate. By the turn of the 19th century, the city was breaking through its original borders, with property becoming more valuable by the minute. Eager to cash in, Amos sold off chunks of the land in small lots. He did, however, keep some of the property in the family. He passed his portion of the Warren estate to a relative, Charles Christopher Amos. The new owner assigned his three-name moniker to a trio of roads that passed through his land. Charles and Christopher (formerly Skinner Road) streets still exist, while Amos Street is now 10th Street. By the 1820s, Christopher Street was a bustling commercial thoroughfare, which it continues to be to this day.

People think New York is this big city where no one knows each other. But when you live in the Village, it's the opposite.

—Nigel Barker

{ Marie's Crisis Cafe }

Tucked away in the large basement of a black-, white- and red-clad building on Grove Street is Marie's Crisis Cafe—opened in 1929 by Marie DuMont as a restaurant with piano music for West Village bohemians. The "Crisis" in the name is a nod to the historic site; Founding Father Thomas Paine, author of "The American Crisis," a series of pamphlets printed during the American Revolution, died in a house formerly located on the lot.

Today, the space lives on as a no-frills piano bar, where professional singers, avid theatergoers and everyone in between have been belting out the best of Broadway show tunes for more than four decades. Of particular interest is the WPA mural behind the bar, its origin unknown.

I am walking in a dream, the aftermath of what I saw and heard at your Cherry Lane Theatre last evening . . . It is so far above the commercial theatre that I tremble to think it may fade and disappear.

—William Carlos Williams

{ Cherry Lane Theatre }

Words by F. Scott Fitzgerald, Eugene O'Neill, Gertrude Stein, Edward Albee, Sam Shepard and David Mamet have leapt off the page and onto the stage of the Cherry Lane Theatre in the West Village. But before becoming a downtown destination for the city's theater community, the 1836 building was a brewery, tobacco warehouse and box factory. Theater artists purchased the edifice in 1924 and transformed it into a playhouse, where experimental theater movements such as The Living Theatre and Theatre of the Absurd took shape. Today, the Off-Broadway venue's 179-seat mainstage and intimate studio space present works by emerging playwrights.

Greenwich Village ... the village of low rents and high arts.
—*O. Henry*

{ 102 Bedford Street }

While strolling in Greenwich Village, you'll notice that the twin-peaked townhouse at 102 Bedford Street looks quite different from its neighbors. Once an 1830 Federal-style house, it was transformed into a 10-unit, five-story apartment building in 1926 that is reminiscent of a Swiss chalet. In the building's heyday, Cary Grant, Douglas Fairbanks, Miles Davis and Walt Disney called the tiny 20-by-18-foot units home.

You can learn more about human nature by reading the Bible than by living in New York.

—*William Lyon Phelps*

{ The Church of St. Luke in the Fields }

The brick, Federal-style Episcopal chapel, named for the patron saint of doctors, opened in 1821. Clement Clarke Moore, author of the poem "'Twas the Night Before Christmas," was a founding warden.

Saint Luke's holds weekday and Sunday services, hosts community events and energetically supports the LGBTQ community. The church's gardens offer a tranquil respite.

Sleep with me sleep with my dogs.
—Sinclair Lewis

{ 69 Charles Street }

Many notable West Village residents have called the buildings along Charles Street home, including Mayor Fiorello LaGuardia, crime novelist James Cain and singer Woody Guthrie. Before Sinclair Lewis found fame as a Nobel Prize-winning novelist, he lived at 69 Charles Street from 1910 to 1913 while working as a copywriter and editor at the city's publishing houses.

Theodosia Burr's Ghost and One if by Land, Two if by Sea

Located in a mid-18th-century carriage house, this charming West Village eatery is one of the most romantic, and haunted, restaurants in the city. If you find it difficult to snag a table, that's because the destination fills up quickly with lovebirds—and approximately 20 ghosts. Skeptical? Just ask the staff. Employees have seen strange things in the historic space, from frames tilting and plates flying to equipment turning on and off inexplicably.

Vice President Aaron Burr owned the building during the 1790s when he was New York's attorney general, so it's no wonder his apparition haunts the halls. Less easily explained is the presence of his daughter, Theodosia. In December 1812, she left her South Carolina home to visit her father in New York. She never made it. Reports claim that pirates kidnapped her. In 1869, a mentally ill woman believed to be Theodosia was spotted living with a couple in North Carolina. When they found her decades earlier stranded on the shore, a portrait of Burr's daughter was her only possession.

At the restaurant, you'll feel Theodosia's unearthly presence in the mezzanine. Other ghosts include a Ziegfeld Follies performer and a woman who always walks down (never up) the stairs.

The Nags Head Portrait of Theodosia Burr

One if by Land, Two if by Sea: 17 Barrow St, New York

I believe in New Yorkers. Whether they've ever questioned the dream in which they live, I wouldn't know, because I won't ever dare ask that question.

—Dylan Thomas

{ White Horse Tavern }

The White Horse Tavern deserves its place in history as New York's most popular hangout for 1950s-era writers (and hardcore drinkers) like Dylan Thomas and Jack Kerouac, who were frequent patrons. Portraits of poet Thomas, who died after a marathon bender at the White Horse, adorn the walls, while outside a plaque commemorates his time spent at the Greenwich Village mainstay. Hunter S. Thompson, James Baldwin, Norman Mailer and an almost never-ending list of influential scribes also enjoyed stiff drinks and lively conversation in the watering hole, whose brews, bar bites and bonhomie continue to attract bookworms and would-be novelists.

To me, a building—if it's beautiful—
is the love of one man, he's made it out
of his love for space, materials, things
like that.

—Martha Graham

{ Westbeth–Bell Laboratories Building }

Between 1898 and 1966, in a collection of 13 buildings in the West Village, technology innovator Bell Telephone Laboratories developed talking movies, phonograph records and transistors, and made the first commercial broadcast.

Four years after Bell Labs moved out, the complex was reborn as the Westbeth Artists Community—providing affordable housing, studios and rehearsal space for visual and performing artists such as painter Robert De Niro Sr., photographer Diane Arbus and actor Vin Diesel. Westbeth is also home to an art gallery, an LGBTQ synagogue and the Martha Graham Center of Contemporary Dance.

East Village

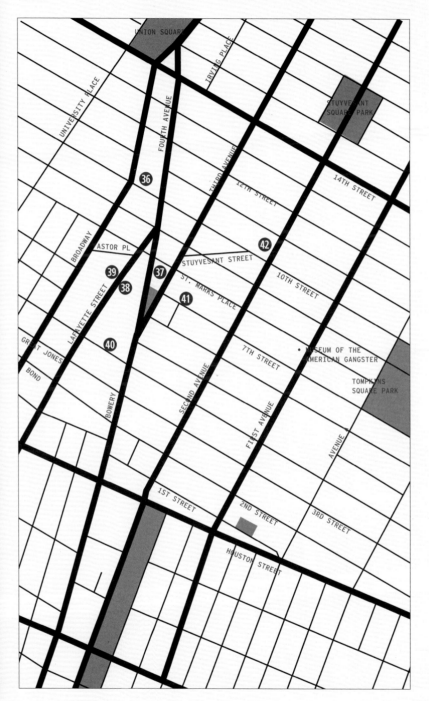

The most wonderful street in the universe is Broadway. It is a world within itself. High and low, rich and poor, pass along at a rate peculiar to New York, and positively bewildering to a stranger."

—Frank Rich

{ Grace Church }

When tapped to spearhead construction of Grace Church, James Renwick Jr.—a 24-year-old architect with few projects under his belt (he'd recently completed a supervisory gig on the 42nd Street Croton Reservoir)—had never built anything before. His first commission, the Gothic landmark on Broadway between East 10th and East 11th streets, opened in 1846. A decade later, he would go on to design arguably one of the city's most famous temples, St. Patrick's Cathedral in Midtown.

General Tom Thumb Wedding in 1863

Although Grace Church looks a lot different than it did in Renwick's day (today's colorful stained-glass windows were tinted glass then; the marble steeple, which splices through the air like a phoenix against its low-lying neighbors, was made of wood; and the lone statuary was a Christ figure in the east window), the church has been a gathering place for the community since its first service.

In 1863, circus owner P.T. Barnum's famous dwarf performer General Tom Thumb (born Charles Sherwood Stratton) married his blushing bride, short-statured starlet Lavinia Warren, in the house of worship, much to the dismay of guests and nosy onlookers.

Today, you can visit the East Village church to hear engaging sermons and its choirs perform free concerts.

John Jacob Astor and His Family

German-born John Jacob Astor came to New York to find his fortune and, in the process, created a business empire and founded one of the most prominent families of the 19th century.

Astor settled in America in 1784 with a few flutes to sell (he had made musical instruments in London) and $25 in his pocket. A few years later, he moved to New York City and opened his own fur shop, often traversing the wilderness for goods. He acquired more shops and merged them into the profitable American Fur Company in 1808. His company, a bond deal with the U.S. government after the War of 1812 and savvy New York real estate investments made him one of the richest men in the country.

Astor's offspring (he had seven children) and their descendants also contributed to the city's growth and cultural significance. Of particular interest, his son William Backhouse Astor Sr. worked in the family business and helped form the Astor Library (later part of the New York Public Library), while his grandsons opened the Waldorf and Astoria hotels, later joined to form the venerable Waldorf-Astoria.

Although the family tree has declined, the Astors' lasting impact on the city remains.

John Jacob Astor, with rifle, obtaining furs for an employer during the early years of his career

Let us have faith that right makes might, and in that faith, let us, to the end, dare to do our duty as we understand it.

—Abraham Lincoln's Cooper Institute Address

{ The Cooper Union Foundation Building }

In the 1850s, liberal-leaning Peter Cooper, founder of The Copper Union, a once tuition-free university open to men and women regardless of race and class, needed a building to house his avant-garde temple of higher learning. Since its 1859 inception, the institution's Italianate brownstone Foundation Building has been the setting of spirited collegiate debates, tension-fueled political demonstrations and everything in between. The landmark's Great Hall has hosted many historical events: Susan B. Anthony and Elizabeth Cady Stanton rallied for women's rights; a young, lanky, unknown attorney from Illinois by the name of Abraham Lincoln gave his first speech in New York to the Young Men's Republic Union; and the NAACP's first meeting took place in the space.

When you are growing up there are two
institutional places that affect you most
powerfully: the church, which belongs
to God, and the public library, which
belongs to you.

—Keith Richards

{ Astor Library }

When John Jacob Astor died in 1848, he left $400,000 to establish a reference library for New York. The Alexander Saeltzer-designed, Rundbogenstil-style building opened in today's East Village in 1854. The collection included thousands of volumes on various subjects, notably sizable selections of linguistics, science and American history books. By the end of the century, the library was experiencing financial difficulties, and its holdings were merged with Lenox Library and the Tilden Trust to form the New York Public Library.

In the 1960s, the building was transformed into The Public Theater, with the musical "Hair" as its first show.

I'll build sometime or other a greater house than any of these, and in this very street.

—*John Jacob Astor*

{ Colonnade Row }

Fronted by a series of two-story-high Corinthian columns and boasting luxuries like indoor plumbing and central heating, the 1833 terrace of nine 26-room Greek Revival-style homes on Lafayette Street in the East Village housed the city's elite. Early tenants of the 27-foot-wide domiciles were John Jacob Astor II, Julia Gardiner (who would marry President John Tyler), Cornelius Vanderbilt and Washington Irving.

Manhattan's Most Haunted House
—*The New York Times*

{ Merchant's House }

Merchant's House, a Federal-style, red brick and white marble rowhouse built in 1832, was occupied by the Tredwells, a wealthy merchant family, for nearly a century, beginning in 1835. After Gertrude Tredwell, who was born in the house in 1840, died in an upstairs bedroom in 1933, the house became a museum, whose Greek Revival rooms remain as they were when the Tredwells lived there.

Art is the response of the living to life. It is therefore the record left behind by civilization.

—John Sloan

{ McSorley's Old Ale House }

Although the sign outside the East Village watering hole states "1854," the year McSorley's Old Ale House actually opened is hotly debated. One thing is certain: It was a no-frills tavern by the 1860s and continues to be to this day.

During its history, the bar has been a popular hangout for presidents, authors, musicians and artists, including Ashcan School painter John Sloan. The tavern was near his studio, and he immortalized his time there in the 1912 oil painting "McSorley's Bar" and again in the 1928 piece "McSorley's Saturday Night." The lively venue was also the source of inspiration for E.E. Cummings' poem "Sitting in McSorley's."

Spanning most of its operation, the saloon was off limits to women. That all changed in 1970 when civil rights attorneys Faith Seidenberg and Karen DeCrow took their case to the Supreme Court to get through the doors.

Now open to guys and gals, the cash-only tavern still boasts plenty of Old New York charm, complete with a sawdust-covered floor and historic memorabilia-covered walls. If you're looking for an alternative to the city's over-complicated gastropub menus and odd mixologist creations, you'll find solace at McSorley's. "Light" or "dark" beer are the only options.

Peter Stuyvesant's Pear Tree

Many newcomers to New York bring with them reminders of home, and that's exactly what Peter Stuyvesant did when he traveled to New Amsterdam from Holland in 1647 to assume the position of director-general.

A pear tree sapling was among his belongings, which he planted on his estate in today's East Village. The Dutch lost control to the British in 1664, but Stuyvesant stayed on his bucolic farm until his death eight years later.

The fruit-bearing tree stood on the corner of what would become 13th Street and Third Avenue for more than 200 years, one of the few reminders of the city's Dutch origins. In 1867, a traffic collision toppled the tree.

Today, a plaque hangs on a nearby building commemorating the tree's significance. A new sapling was also planted nearby, hopefully to survive 200 years and beyond—road traffic permitting. You can see a part of the historic tree enclosed in glass at the New-York Historical Society Museum & Library on the Upper West Side.

Peter Stuyvesant, in 1664, standing on shore among residents of New Amsterdam who are pleading with him not to open fire on the British, who have arrived in warships waiting in the harbor to claim the territory for England. —"The Fall of New Amsterdam," J.L.G. Ferris, c. 1932 (left)

Peter Stuyvesant's Pear Tree

Our little force will march on tomorrow or the day after.
—*Peter Stuyvesant*

{ St. Mark's Church in-the-Bowery }

In 1660, Peter Stuyvesant, New Amsterdam's governor, built a family chapel on the current site in the East Village. When he died in 1672, his body was interred in a vault underneath, where it remains to this day. In 1793, the chapel was donated to the Episcopal Church. John McComb Jr.'s Georgian-style church was built on the lot and consecrated in 1799. Stuyvesant's ghost roams the interior.

Lorcan Otway
Curator
Museum of the American Gangster

Even though he was one of the most successful bootleggers in New York City, Frank Hoffman kept a low profile, preferring to use another person, Walter Scheib, as a front man for his illegal activities.

During Prohibition, Hoffman retained his main speakeasy, known as Scheib's Place, by taking out a large number of mortgages on the property under his own name, as well as the names of members of his bootlegging cartel and two corporations of which his wife and he were the corporate officers. The corporations were named Rio Realty and Rita Holding. This was an inside joke as "Rio Rita" was the name of a 1927 musical, produced by Florenz Ziegfeld, about a bootlegger who falls in love with a Hispanic nightclub singer.

To an investigator today, it is as if Hoffman drew a road map to his front door. But it was good his scheme of hiding behind a smoke screen of paper worked, because the foundations of the speakeasy were packed with dynamite, ready to blow up the building if the club was raided and Hoffman needed a cover for his getaway with millions of dollars. The triggers to this booby trap can still be seen during tours of the Museum of the American Gangster, housed at 80 Saint Marks Place in the former Scheib's Place.

In 1964, two million dollars of Hoffman's money was discovered by my father, Howard Otway, and me in a basement bunker of the building that Dad had bought from Scheib. Dad gave the money to Scheib, but it was tainted money. As it turns out, Hoffman disappeared forever on the night of November 7, 1945, most likely murdered by an associate, who also killed his Hispanic nightclub singer girlfriend, Ghia Ortega.

Museum of the American Gangster: 80 St. Marks Place, New York

Union Square, Gramercy Park, Madison Suare

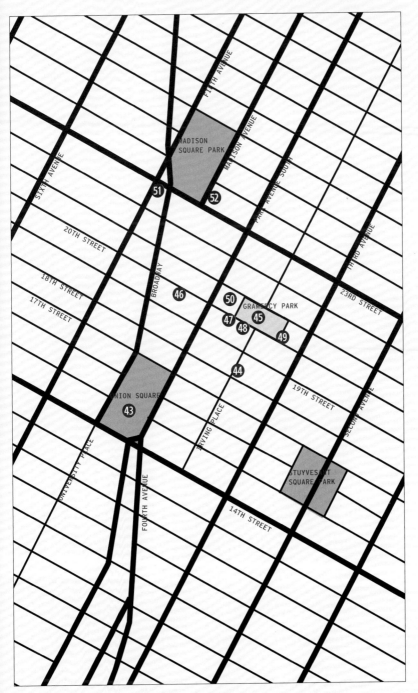

And New York is the most beautiful city in the world? It is not far from it. No urban night is like the night there . . . Squares after squares of flame, set up and cut into the aether. Here is our poetry, for we have pulled down the stars to our will.

—Ezra Pound

{ Union Square }

Union Square opened as Union Place in 1839, named after the intersection, or "union", of Bloomingdale Road (now Broadway) and Bowery Road (Fourth Avenue). Frederick Law Olmsted and Calvert Vaux later redesigned the square, widening sidewalks and removing a fence, to make it more accessible for mass gatherings.

The green space has changed a lot since then but it still retains Olmsted and Vaux's original intent. It was the site of the first Labor Day celebration in 1882, when 10,000 workers passed through. Today, it hosts labor and political rallies, religious meetings, hippies, vendors and skateboarders.

It'll be a great place if they ever finish it.

—O. Henry

{ Pete's Tavern }

Opening at the end of the Civil War and masquerading as a flower shop during Prohibition, Pete's Tavern has been a popular Gramercy District pub since 1864. Ex-con, heavy drinker and author O. Henry was a frequenter and allegedly wrote "The Gift of the Magi" in the front booth. Nowadays, the pub restaurant serves Italian-American food and is notable for its convivial happy hour.

New York [cannot] remain the center of commerce and capital for this continent, unless it has an independent bar and an honest judiciary.

—*Samuel J. Tilden*

{ Gramercy Park }

Two-acre Gramercy Park, roughly bordered by outlying East 21st and East 20th streets to the north and south and Third Avenue and Park Avenue South to the east and west, is the only private park in Manhattan.

Seeing the success of private squares in Savannah, land developer Samuel B. Ruggles envisioned an exclusive sojourn for New York's wealthiest citizens. In the early 1830s, he began the lofty task of transforming a muddy creek into today's Gramercy Park—dividing the land into 42 lots for the actual park and 66 lots for surrounding urban palaces.

When the gated grassy grounds opened almost a decade

Gramercy Park,
East 19th Street and
Irving Place

later, the first residents of the Italianate and Greek Revival mansions along the perimeter included architects Stanford White and Richard Morris Hunt and authors Edith Wharton and Herman Melville. Actor Edwin Booth set up The Players Club at 16 Gramercy Park and lived there for the last five years of his life. A large statue of the thespian is firmly fixed in the middle of the park.

Keys are only given to those who live in buildings facing the green space, but if you want to take a stroll, guests of nearby Gramercy Park Hotel are permitted inside.

There was also a Russian moujik drawing a gilt sledge on a piece of malachite.

—Theodore Roosevelt

{ Teddy Roosevelt House }

Theodore Roosevelt was one of New York's most influential residents. Before becoming president, he was the city's police commissioner, a New York assemblyman and later governor of New York State. The future 26th president of the United States was born in a four-story brownstone in the Gramercy Park neighborhood in 1858 and lived there until he was 15. The historic house is now a museum.

'Then stay with me a little longer,'
Madame Olenska said in a low
tone, just touching his knee with her
plumed fan. It was the lightest touch,
but it thrilled him like a caress.

—Edith Wharton

{ The National Arts Club }

By the 1890s, American artists and writers were turning to their homeland, instead of Europe, for inspiration. In 1898, New York Times art critic Charles de Kay founded The National Arts Club to foster public interests in the arts.

First located in a 34th Street brownstone, the club has occupied the Samuel J. Tilden House since 1906. You can see the Calvert Vaux-designed, Victorian Gothic-style mansion's opulent interiors in Martin Scorsese's "The Age of Innocence" or start the application process to the invitation-only club. If you get in, membership comes with plenty of perks, including a coveted key to Gramercy Park.

An actor is a sculptor who carves in snow.
—Edwin Booth

{ The Players Club }

In 1888, actor Edwin Booth opened The Players at 16 Gramercy Park for the theater community to socialize, choosing the name from a line in Shakespeare's "As You Like It." The private club's membership was exclusively male until it started admitting women on April 23, 1989, The Bard's birthday. Helen Hayes, nicknamed the "First Lady of the American Theater," was its first female member.

I've lived in New York when I've had nothing, and I've lived in New York when I had money ...

—*Richard Gere*

{ 34 Gramercy Park }

The Queen Anne-style 1883 structure, with ornate floral carvings, was the city's first co-op apartment building. The exclusive dwelling faces verdant Gramercy Park, and each resident is given a key to the park, which is off limits to the general public. Richard Gere's flat was once owned by Margaret Hamilton, the Wicked Witch of the West in "The Wizard of Oz."

The starred and stately nights seemed
haughty dames in jewelled velvets,
nursing at home in lonely pride, the
memory of their absent conquering
Earls, the golden helmeted suns!

—Herman Melville

{ 4 Gramercy Park }

Nos. 3 and 4 Gramercy Park look different from their neighbors. The Greek Revival mansions that face the exclusive green space feature combined porches—ornate, cast-iron structures designed by architect Alexander Jackson Davis.

Following the end of his term, NYC Mayor James Harper moved into No. 4. He installed two lampposts at the base of his porch, a custom from the Dutch burgomasters' tradition of placing lanterns in front of their residences that, when lit, let passersby know they were there. Now a status symbol, all New York mayors have the option of installing two gas lanterns outside their homes.

I found myself agape, admiring a sky-scraper the prow of the Flat-iron Building, to be particular, ploughing up through the traffic of Broadway and Fifth Avenue in the afternoon light.

—H.G. Wells,
"The Future in America"

{ Flatiron Building }

Built in 1902 as the Fuller Building, this Daniel Burnham-designed, Beaux Arts-style, Renaissance palazzo structure is one of the world's first skyscrapers. When completed, it was also one the city's tallest buildings. Turn-of-the-last-century New Yorkers were skeptical of its durability—placing bets on how far debris would fall when the structure eventually toppled. With a strong steel skeleton and limestone and terra-cotta facade, the icon has lasted over a century. The surrounding Flatiron District neighborhood is a nod to its lasting presence. Most of the 21 floors house offices, but there are street-level shops and an art gallery in the prow.

New York is to the nation what the white church spire is to the village – the visible symbol of aspiration and faith, the white plume saying the way is up.

—E.B. White

{ Met Life Tower }

Often overshadowed by the Flatiron Building, Met Life Tower is another notable structure that keeps watchful eye over Madison Square Park. Designed by Napoleon LeBrun & Sons, the four-faced clock tower, with the diameter of each timepiece stretching 26.5 feet and each minute hand weighing half a ton, was the tallest building in the world when it was completed in 1909.

Inspired by St. Mark's Campanile in Venice, the historic column was an addition to the 11-story Metropolitan Life Insurance headquarters. Credit Suisse now occupies the building's base, while a luxury hotel and restaurant are located in the spire. The roof is illuminated nightly.

Two Towers, Alfred Stieglitz, 1914

Chelsea, Midtown South

The stockings were hung by the chimney with care,
In hopes that St. Nicholas soon would be there.

—Clement Clarke Moore

{ General Theological Seminary }

Chelsea's General Theological Seminary is a tranquil retreat from the noise, hustle and bustle of the surrounding city. Built on a former apple orchard owned by "A Visit From St. Nicholas" author and professor Clement Clarke Moore, the Greek Revival buildings were crafted by George Coolidge Haight between 1883 and 1902. The structures hide the breathtaking quadrangle from the city streets.

In need of funds in recent years, the Seminary has leased some of its buildings for commercial and residential use. To enter the enclave, look for the main entrance on West 21st Street, halfway between Ninth and 10th avenues.

I had no concept of what life at the Chelsea Hotel would be like when we checked in, but I soon realized it was a tremendous stroke of luck to end up there.

—Patti Smith

{ Chelsea Hotel }

Built between 1884 and 1885 as an apartment co-op, the 12-story, brick edifice on West 23rd Street was reborn as a bohemian hotel a few decades later. Since then, it's been home to a variety of artists, actors, musicians and authors.

Andy Warhol documented the lives of his All-Stars who lived there in "Chelsea Girls," while Stanley Kubrick penned the screenplay of "2001: A Space Odyssey" and soon-to-be-famous artists hung works in the stairwell. The hotel has also seen its share of somber times: Author Charles R. Jackson attempted suicide in his room, and Sid Vicious' girlfriend, Nancy Spungen, was murdered in theirs.

We are coming, Father Abraham, three hundred thousand more ...

—James Sloan Gibbons

{ Lamartine Place }

Built in 1846, the charming rowhouses on West 29th Street, between Eighth and Ninth avenues, situated on what was then called Lamartine Place, were associated with several well-known abolitionist families during the American Civil War, including Abigail Hopper Gibbons and her father, Isaac T. Hopper, who lived at No. 337. The latter is considered the father of the Underground Railroad. During the 1856 Anti-Slavery Convention, black and white guests were invited to stay at the historic home; in 1859, Abigail met with abolitionist John Brown there. The structure was damaged during the Emancipation Proclamation celebrations in 1862 and was burned

New York Draft Ri[...]
in 1863

during the New York City Civil War Draft Riots the following year. The Gibbons' daughters narrowly escaped the angry mob by climbing over the rooftops of neighboring homes to their uncle Samuel Brown's house at No. 335. Other area residents weren't so lucky; Samuel Sinclair at No. 353, publisher of the New York Tribune, was attacked when rumors swirled that well-known abolitionist and Tribune founder Horace Greeley lived there. Heavily modified from their original Greek Revival facades, many houses on the block are taller and now feature Renaissance Revival cornices. No. 341 most resembles the original design.

Lost New York:
Tin Pan Alley

Cluttered today with wholesale shops, 28th Street between Fifth and Sixth avenues was the epicenter of the city's songwriting industry in the late 19th and early 20th centuries—a stretch dominated by music publishers and demonstration rooms. The clamor of piano sounds emanating from the buildings prompted New York Herald journalist Monroe Rosenfeld to describe the area as Tin Pan Alley. The nickname was later used to describe the era's music in general. Dwindling sheet-music sales and the emergence of new genres ended Tin Pan Alley. A commemorative plaque is near the corner of West 28th Street and Broadway.

Tin Pan Alley's most famous composer, Irving Berlin, 1906

Buildings along Tin Pan Alley, c. 1905

One can't paint New York as it is,
but rather as it is felt.

—Georgia O'Keeffe

{ 69th Regiment Armory }

Built in 1906 as a training facility and marshaling center for the National Guard, the 69th Regiment Armory housed the 1913 International Exhibition of Modern Art, the first major exhibition of contemporary art in America. The event introduced Western artists and audiences to European styles like Cubism. Works by Paul Cézanne, Marcel Duchamp and Pablo Picasso, among others, were on display.

In subsequent years, it hosted roller derbies, New York Knicks games and a Victoria's Secret fashion show. Today, it's the 69th Regiment's headquarters and houses Civil War-era flags and a handwritten letter from President Lincoln.

I may be president of the United States, but my private life is nobody's damned business.

—*Chester A. Arthur*

{ Chester A. Arthur Home }

President Chester A. Arthur lived in a townhouse at 123 Lexington Avenue. When he was vice president, he stayed here after the July 2, 1881, assassination attempt on President James Garfield. When Garfield died from his wounds on September 19, Arthur took the oath of office as the nation's 21st president in the townhouse's parlor. A Mediterranean grocer and apartments now occupy the historic space.

Josh Vogel
Gallery Manager
The Skyscraper Museum

One of my favorite Art Deco skyscrapers in NYC has a scale model of itself above its entrances! The 12-foot version of 70 Pine (formerly the Cities Services, then American International Building) is carved in stone on the north and south facades. At the bottom of the stone model is a tinier version: the scale model of the model! [Also of interest] the original plan for the Met Life North building, now known as Eleven Madison, proposed by architect Harvey Wiley Corbett in 1928, would have been a 100-story tower that dominated the Midtown skyline. However, after the stock market crash in 1929, Met Life decided to stop at the 32-story base.

The Skyscraper Museum:
39 Battery Place, New York

*The Empire State, a lonely
dinosaur, rose sadly at midtown,
highest tower, tallest mountain,
longest road, King Kong's eyrie,
meant to moor airships, alas.*

—Vincent Scully

{ Empire State Building }

The William F. Lamb-designed, Art Deco Empire State Building rests on the original site of the Waldorf-Astoria hotel and took a little over a year to complete, competing with rapid construction of the Chrysler Building across town and 40 Wall Street to the south for the title of "World's Tallest Building."

Ground broke on January 22, 1930, with over 3,000 men working at lightning speed to erect four-and-a-half stories per week. When President Herbert Hoover presided over the ribbon-cutting on May 1, 1931, the 1,250-foot, 102-story structure reigned as the tallest in the world—holding the honor for nearly

*A construction work[er]
at the Empire State
Building, around
1930*

40 years before being surpassed by the World Trade Center in 1970.

Still one of the most recognizable skyscrapers to grace the Manhattan cityscape, the icon has starred in over 250 films and houses so many companies it has its own ZIP code.

You can dance to live saxophone music on the 86th-floor observation deck or head to the 102nd-floor observatory and take in expansive, bird's-eye views of Manhattan, New Jersey, Pennsylvania, Connecticut and Massachusetts. Back inside, the renovated Art Deco lobby is also worth a gander; it's one of the few NYC interiors with historic landmark status.

Astor 400 and
Waldorf-Astoria Hotel

The Astor family was a large brood, but there could only be one "Mrs. Astor," and that distinction eventually fell on the shoulders of Caroline Webster "Lina" Schermerhorn.

She married William Backhouse Astor Jr. in 1853. Later, she served as the family's matriarch, holding invitation-only soirees attended by 400 citizens she deemed to be members of the city's aristocracy.

Caroline lived in a mansion at 350 Fifth Avenue, next door to her husband's older brother John Jacob Astor III. When her brother-in-law died in 1890, her nephew William Waldorf Astor, now the male head of the family, felt his wife, Mary "Mamie" Dahlgren Paul, should hold the title of "Mrs. Astor." Caroline used her social clout to prevent the change, but her nephew

The Waldorf-Astoria on 34th Street and Fifth Avenue, c. 1902

got his revenge. He tore down his father's mansion and erected a luxe hotel, the Waldorf, on the lot. At the time, hotels weren't frequented by polite society, so this was the ultimate insult.

Caroline eventually moved uptown, and her son razed her property and built an even grander hotel of his own, the Astoria, in its place. The hotels later merged to form the Waldorf-Astoria. Both properties were torn down in 1928 to clear space for the Empire State Building.

He started seven failed business before finally hitting big with his store, Macy's, in New York City.

—Evan Carmichael

{ Macy's Herald Square }

Macy's Herald Square flagship is the store's second location. It opened in 1858 on 14th Street and Sixth Avenue and moved to 34th Street in 1902, expanding to Seventh Avenue two decades later. Today, it's the country's largest department store, with 11 levels and two million square feet of retail space.

The first building in the country to have modern escalators when it opened, you can ride 43 of the original wooden contraptions on the store's Broadway side. Long associated with the holidays, Macy's premiered its Thanksgiving Day Parade in 1924, while the emporium's window displays have dazzled passersby since its days downtown.

*[Slogan of her 'Trouble Bureau' for
needy artists and musicians:] Happiness
is a change of trouble.*

—Malvina Hoffman

{ Sniffen Court }

Peppered among Manhattan's sprawling thoroughfares and high-rises are hidden courtyards, many unknown to even longtime city dwellers. Nestled on East 36th Street, between Third and Lexington avenues in Murray Hill, is Sniffen Court. Built by John Sniffen in 1850 as stables for townhouses, the structures were converted into residences in the early 1900s.

Sculptors Harriet Whitney Frishmuth and Malvina Hoffman (known for creating the Field Museum's Hall of Man) lived there. The latter's plaques of horsemen are still in the courtyard. The secluded setting appears on the Doors' "Strange Days" album cover.

The key to living a moral life is this: Do nothing in private that you would be ashamed to discuss openly with your mother.

—J.P. Morgan

{ The Morgan Library }

John Pierpont "J.P." Morgan, a shrewd financier in the late 19th and early 20th centuries, was an avid collector.

In 1906, a Classical Revival, palazzo-like private library and study was built to house his vast collection of fine art, rare books, manuscripts and ancient artifacts.

In 1924, John Pierpont Morgan Jr. opened his father's library, complete with grand fireplace and rich tapestries, to the public. Today, the museum complex includes the original library building, an annex on the site of Morgan's home, the brownstone where Morgan Jr. lived, a garden court and a Renzo Piano-designed pavilion.

I think the New York Public Library is so, so amazing. It's literally the coolest place – It's good shelter from the sun and it's the most beautiful building. It's really, really fun.

—Natalie Portman

{ New York Public Library }

By the end of the 19th century, New York City was becoming one of the world's most distinguished metropolises. It surpassed Paris by population and catered to citizens' cultural needs with dozens of theaters and The Metropolitan Museum of Art. Former New York Governor Samuel J. Tilden believed a world-class library and reading room would fit nicely with the city's offerings.

A merger of the Tilden Trust, Astor and Lenox libraries, the New York Public Library was established in 1895. The cornerstone of the Carrère and Hastings-designed, Beaux Arts-style fortress (on the site of the Croton Reservoir) was

Croton Reservoir, 18[...]

laid in May 1902. Construction took almost a decade to complete and, at the time, was the largest marble structure ever attempted in the country.

President William Taft presided over the opening ceremony on May 23, 1911, and the next day, the public institution welcomed between 30,000 and 50,000 New Yorkers. With a picturesque place next to Bryant Park, the Midtown beauty's most prominent statues are Edward Clark Potter's Patience and Fortitude figures, two imposing marble lions bookending the Fifth Avenue steps.

Today, the building is the main branch of the city's comprehensive library system and has been featured on both the small and silver screens.

New York has a trip-hammer vitality which drives you insane with restlessness, if you have no inner stabilizer ... In New York I have always felt lonely, the loneliness of the caged animal, which brings on crime, sex, alcohol and other madnesses.

—Henry Miller

Midtown

Today I arrived by train in New York City, which I'd never seen before, walked through the grandeur of Grand Central Terminal, stepped outside, got my first look at the city and instantly fell in love with it. Silently, inside myself, I yelled: I should have been born here!

—*Edward Robb Ellis*

{ Grand Central Terminal }

The massive Midtown East transportation hub began life in the 1870s as a train depot for three separate rail lines. By 1900, it was rebuilt as "Grand Central Station," with an enormous train shed that rivaled the Eiffel Tower for 19th-century engineering supremacy. Soon after, work on today's Grand Central Terminal was underway.

Cornelius Vanderbilt's 10-year endeavor opened on February 2, 1913, welcoming over 150,000 visitors. Over the next few decades, it housed an art gallery, school, museum and movie theater, while 65 million commuters traveled its rails. Today, Metro-North whisks 750,000 people daily to New York's northern counties and Connecticut.

The beautiful Beaux Arts facade is topped with a 50-foot-high sculpture of three Greek gods surrounding the largest Tiffany clock in the world. The interior teems with winding corridors, shops, restaurants and bars, a whispering gallery and a tennis court in the Annex. The cathedral-like Main Concourse boasts a glistening four-faced gold Tiffany clock at its center. Look closely at the vaulted ceiling of zodiac constellations (installed backward), and you'll see a hole from which a wire was hung to support the 1957 Redstone rocket. You'll also notice a lone dirty brick, a throwback to how the nicotine-covered ceiling looked before restoration.

Cornelius "Commodore" Vanderbilt

Cornelius Vanderbilt, between 1844 and 1860

Cornelius "Commodore" Vanderbilt's shrewd business tactics transformed his shipping and railroad companies into multimillion-dollar industries and made him one of the richest men in the country, worth more than $100 million when he died in 1877 at the age of 82.

Like many poor families in early-19th-century New York, Vanderbilt received only a few years of formal education, working instead with his father ferrying goods between their native Staten Island to Manhattan on the family's sailboat. As a teenager, he transported cargo on his own vessel, later acquiring a respectable fleet and learning more about steamboats. He worked for a wealthy steamship operator for a few years before branching out on his own, operating steamship ferry service along New York waterways and engaging in fare wars with competitors.

Vanderbilt was in his 70s when he began to build his railroad empire—buying small lines, pouncing on rivals when their shares were low, and expanding and merging his holdings to create a dynasty. Knowing the city would eventually move north, he built Grand Central Depot on the outskirts of town. The space was rebuilt in 1913 as Grand Central Terminal, but Vanderbilt, having died three decades earlier, never got to see it.

I get out of the taxi and it's probably the only city which in reality looks better than on the postcards, New York.

—*Miloš Forman*

{ Chrysler Building }

This Art Deco masterpiece in Midtown, designed by William Van Alen and financed by automotive executive Walter P. Chrysler, was part of a highly publicized competition to build the world's tallest skyscraper. Ground broke on September 19, 1928, with an average of four floors completed per week. The spire was constructed in secret and installed in 90 minutes. Upon completion in May of 1930, the 1,048-foot, 77-story, steel-supported brick building reigned as the tallest in the world (and the first fully air-conditioned skyscraper), only to be surpassed by the Empire State Building 11 months later.

Although Chrysler never owned the building, it did house his company's headquarters from 1930 to the mid-1950s. Nods to the 1929 model cars are featured on the facade: 61st-floor corners have eagles (replicas of hood ornaments), while radiator cap replicas are perched on 31st-floor corners. Also of note, the crown is composed of seven radiating terraced arches, resembling a sunburst.

Inside, the first two floors of the lobby housed an automobile showroom. The members-only Cloud Club occupied floors 66 through 68, while a public viewing gallery was on the 71st floor. All early features are long gone. Today, various offices occupy the building.

New York Draft Riots, 1863

Confederate sympathies regarding New York's involvement in the cotton trade, coupled with working-class whites' fears of competing for jobs with emancipated blacks, fueled the four days of rioting that ravaged the city in the summer of 1863.

In March, Congress passed the Enrollment Act, supplying the Union with more troops during the Civil War. Tensions reached boiling point on July 13, the draft's second day, when a heated crowd of mainly Irish laborers attacked the draft headquarters at Third Avenue and 47th Street. With federal troops and the New York militia battling the national conflict, only the NYPD was left to quell the city's unrest. The department proved too small to squash the riot, and the mob moved through the area like wildfire, torching the mayor's residence and police stations, and vandalizing many more buildings. Rioting resumed the next day, with destruction of more homes and businesses.

On the third day, the draft was suspended to appease the crowd. The New York Militia returned the following day to restore order. When the dust finally settled, more than 100 people were killed while thousands more were injured. The city was faced with millions of dollars in property damage, and most of the black population fled to New Jersey and Brooklyn.

Charge of the Police at the Tribune Office, from "Harper's Pictorial History of the Civil War"

A hundred times have I thought New York is a catastrophe, and fifty times: It is a beautiful catastrophe.

—Le Corbusier

{ United Nations Headquarters }

Following World War II, the Allied forces set up the United Nations to replace the League of Nations and prevent war atrocities from ever happening again. First comprised of 51 nations, the U.N. now boasts 193 member states.

The organization's headquarters, where world leaders come together to discuss diplomacy, international security and human rights, was built by a multinational architectural team between 1947 and 1953 on the site of a slaughterhouse. The complex is home to the General Assembly and Security Council.

The 18-acre site, hugging Manhattan's eastern reaches

Turtle Bay in 1931, the land for U.N. headquarters

and resting on international territory, is peppered with several buildings in the modernist, International Style. Most notable are the Secretariat, a 39-story tower featuring the city's first glass curtain wall, and the General Assembly building, with its grand hall often depicted on the silver screen.

Even if you aren't an ambassador, you can still visit the historic setting. The visitor center offers guided tours and exhibitions in public spaces. You can grab a bite to eat in the Delegates Dining Room, with all-encompassing views of the East River, or head outside and see sculptures by Carl Fredrik Reuterswärd and Yevgeny Vuchetich, gardens and member states' flags waving proudly in the wind.

U.N. Deal: Rockefeller and Zeckendorf at Club Monte Carlo, 1946

 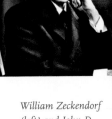

William Zeckendorf (left) and John D. Rockefeller Jr.

In the 1930s, real estate developer William Zeckendorf Sr. began purchasing land along the East River to develop a "city within a city," eventually acquiring 17 acres between 42nd and 48th streets. He tapped Rockefeller Center architect Wallace Harrison to help bring his project to fruition.

Unfortunately, Zeckendorf didn't have the cash for construction. Around the same time, the United Nations was in a hurry to secure a land deal for its headquarters. On December 10, 1946 (the day before deadline), Harrison and Nelson Rockefeller decided Zeckendorf's Turtle Bay property would be the perfect place for the development.

Harrison, with plans in hand, went to work finding Zeckendorf. He eventually tracked him down to Club Monte Carlo, a nightclub Zeckendorf owned on Madison Avenue and East 54th Street. Harrison sat down with the developer, in the midst of throwing a party, and offered him $8.5 million for his property. Zeckendorf said yes, and the two men, along with Zeckendorf's partner Henry Sears, moved to another table to spread out the map. On it, Zeckendorf scribbled "8.5 million— United Nations only. December 10 for 30 days."

Nelson's father, John D. Rockefeller Jr., donated the land to the U.N. for its headquarters.

*In leaving Hollywood and coming to New York,
I feel I can be more myself.* —*Marilyn Monroe*

{ Waldorf-Astoria Hotel }

The Waldorf Astoria began as two German Renaissance-style
hotels built by competitive Astor cousins. The Waldorf and
The Astoria merged into The Waldorf-Astoria in 1897. The
hotel relocated to Park Avenue in 1931 to make way for the
Empire State Building and eventually dropped the hyphen.
Every president since Herbert Hoover has stayed there.
Marilyn Monroe called it home.

I'll have more than Astor, by Christ!

—Cornelius Vanderbilt

{ St. Bartholomew's Church }

St. Bartholomew's began its life downtown in 1835. The church relocated uptown to Madison Avenue in 1872—designed by architect James Renwick and later embellished with a portal by Stanford White—to serve its congregation.

When Renwick's building fell into disrepair, architect Bertram Goodhue designed a new Romanesque-style church on Park Avenue between East 50th and East 51st streets. The current building still retains White's portal. Opened in 1918, Goodhue's masterpiece features an impressive Byzantine-style, mosaic-clad interior. The cinematic setting was featured in the 1981 film "Arthur" and its remake.

I try to be a good shiksa wife. I go to Central Synagogue in New York.

—Drew Barrymore

{ Central Synagogue }

On Lexington Avenue, Central Synagogue's exotic facade, with ornate Moorish towers and sparkling domes, seems peculiar against a backdrop of minimalist Midtown skyscrapers. Built in 1872 by architect Henry Fernbach, the Moorish Revival-style temple is one of the oldest buildings on the block and one of the oldest synagogues in the country.

A reinterpretation of Budapest's famed Dohány Street Synagogue, the structure is a homage to the Jews who once lived in Moorish Spain. The synagogue also owns the Salem Fields Cemetery, Brooklyn, where many of the Guggenheims, Foxes (of 20th Century Fox) and Shuberts (of Shubert theaters) are buried.

You won't see any more private mansions like this.
—Fiorella La Guardia

{ Villard Houses }

In 1881, Henry Villard, president of the Northern Pacific Railway, tapped McKim, Mead and White to build six Italian Renaissance-style mansions on Madison Avenue. Since 1884, the palatial pads have served as private residences, lodgings for World War II servicewomen and office space. The exteriors were featured on "Gossip Girl" as the hotel where the van der Woodsen family lived.

When I was a girl, my grandmother would take me during the holidays to see the windows at Saks and Rockefeller Center.

—Michael Learned

{ Rockefeller Center }

In the late 1920s, John D. Rockefeller Jr. wanted to develop a "city within a city." By 1939, his vision had come to fruition.

Originally featuring 14 buildings built between 1931 and 1939—the famous "Lunch Atop a Skyscraper" photo was taken during construction—the Art Deco complex's most celebrated structures are 30 Rockefeller Plaza and Radio City Music Hall.

The former features a breathtaking lobby, shops, restaurants and an ice-skating rink. Many companies have occupied the offices, including early tenants Newsweek and the Radio Corporation of America.

Radio City Music Hall's first decades saw theatergoers watch live shows, while moviegoers

Lunch atop a Skyscraper
(30 Rockefeller Plaza)
1932

later on enjoyed the premieres of "King Kong" and "Breakfast at Tiffany's."

Today, the complex still bustles with activity. NBC broadcasts "Saturday Night Live" from its 30 Rock studios, while the 65th-floor Rainbow Room is one of the most-coveted dining reservations in town. The observation decks on the 67th, 69th and 70th floors offer panoramic views of the city.

Visitors flock to see the Rockettes dance at Radio City Music Hall during the "Christmas Spectacular," a tradition since 1932. Another custom is the lighting of the Rockefeller Center Christmas Tree, first established by the complex's construction workers in 1931.

Arrival of Rockefeller

John D. Rockefeller Sr., 1885

John D. Rockefeller Sr. was already an oil tycoon when he moved his family to New York City in 1883, settling into a mansion at 4 West 54th Street.

Born in Richford, New York, he moved often as a youngster, eventually planting roots in Cleveland, Ohio, and establishing an oil refinery in the area. Through careful business investments, he bought out competitors to form Standard Oil Company. In 1885, he moved his empire's headquarters to 26 Broadway, an Ebenezer L. Roberts-designed, neoclassical building in the heart of the Financial District.

Although Rockefeller's time in New York was marred by legal troubles— his trips in and out of court due to antitrust legislation routinely made headlines— his philanthropic efforts contributed greatly to the city's advancement.

After dissolving his corporation into smaller companies, he dedicated the remainder of his life to charitable pursuits, giving more than $530 million to several causes. He helped found the Rockefeller Institute for Medical Research (now Rockefeller University) on the Upper East Side and the Rockefeller Foundation, which to this day funds medical studies and education. Future generations built the commercial complex Rockefeller Center in the heart of Midtown and helped finance construction of the United Nations headquarters.

I love the city in an emotional, irrational way, like loving your mother or your father even though they're a drunk or a thief. I've loved the city my whole life—to me, it's like a great woman.

—Woody Allen

{ St. Patrick's Cathedral }

Archbishop John Hughes wanted to build a larger St. Patrick's Cathedral to replace the church on Mulberry Street. Work began in 1858, but the American Civil War put a pin in the project. James Renwick Jr.'s Gothic Revival masterpiece finally opened in 1879.

Robert Kennedy and Babe Ruth's funerals were held in the cathedral, while F. Scott and Zelda Fitzgerald got hitched in the adjoining rectory. Pope Francis delivered a homily in the cathedral when he visited the city in 2015. New York's archbishops are laid to rest in a crypt behind the high altar. Former Haitian slave and church benefactor Pierre Toussaint is the only non-clergyman interred there.

Almost, I am tempted to say, I will believe in God, yes, in spite of the church and the ministers.

—*Thomas Wolfe*

{ Saint Thomas Church }

Although fire destroyed the first three versions, today's Gothic-style Saint Thomas Church has been a Midtown fixture since 1913. The Ralph Adams Cram and Bertram Grosvenor Goodhue-designed building features the largest Great Reredos in the world. Peter Paul Rubens' "The Adoration of the Magi" painting is near the gallery stairs. The Episcopal church's choir of men and boys sings at services and concerts.

Vanderbilt Costume Ball, Monday, March 26, 1883

The fancy dress ball that Alva Vanderbilt threw in the spring of 1883 would put the most luxe shindig you've ever attended to shame.

The wife of William Kissam Vanderbilt had one goal in mind: to be formally recognized by Caroline Astor, the gatekeeper to New York society. Mrs. Astor had strict guidelines as to who was considered part of her circle, and the "new money" Vanderbilts just didn't cut it.

In an effort to get Mrs. Astor's attention, Alva planned the social event of the season, a lavish ball, with the city's most fashionable socialites in attendance. When the time came to send out invitations, Mrs. Astor's daughter Carrie was left off the guest list.

Of course, Mrs. Astor investigated the slight. In response, Alva used the excuse that she had never been called upon by the Astor matriarch, so she didn't know where to send the invitation. This left Mrs. Astor with little choice but to visit Alva's home and leave her calling card, welcoming the Vanderbilts into society.

The ball, held at the Vanderbilt's mansion at 660 Fifth Avenue, was attended by 1,200 guests. Festivities lasted well into the night and cost an estimated $6 million by today's standards.

Vanderbilt's mansion (1898) at 660 Fifth Avenue on 52nd Street and Alva Vanderbilt

I love New York, even though it isn't mine, the way something has to be, a tree or a street or a house, something, anyway, that belongs to me because I belong to it.

—Truman Capote

{ Plaza Hotel }

Sitting on land once occupied by the Fifth Avenue pond, the 19-story Plaza replaced an earlier hotel on the site. Henry Janeway Hardenbergh, the Dakota Apartments' architect, designed and built the lavish lodging, opened in 1907, to resemble a medieval French chateau.

This is where The Beatles stayed during their U.S. debut and Truman Capote held his famous Black and White Ball. Cary Grant was kidnapped from the Oak Room in "North by Northwest" and Macaulay Culkin slid across the lobby floor in "Home Alone 2," revealing a beautiful mosaic under the carpet during filming. You can shop, dine and spend the night.

Yet, as only New Yorkers know, if you can get through the twilight, you'll live through the night. —*Dorothy Parker*

{ The Algonquin Hotel }

This Theater District hotel was a gathering spot for the Vicious Circle (a.k.a. the Algonquin Round Table) group of Roaring Twenties literary elite—Robert Benchley, Robert E. Sherwood, Dorothy Parker, Alexander Woollcott and others— who met daily for lunch and spirited conversation. Today, visitors can grab cocktails at the Blue Bar or pet the Algonquin cat, the hotel's longstanding resident.

Bobby Traversa
Tour Guide
Inside Broadway Tours

Known as the Times Square Church since 1989, 237 West 51st Street was originally designed by Warner Brothers as an ornate movie palace. Between film screenings, lavish live shows often graced its massive stage. Spotting an opportunity, Broadway producer Anthony Brady Farrell purchased the site in 1948, renovating the movie house into a legitimate Broadway theater and renaming it after newspaper critic Mark Hellinger. Many legendary shows graced this stage, including the original productions of "My Fair Lady" and "Sugar Babies." The Hellinger would eventually become the Times Square Church but, in an ironic twist of fate, not before hosting the original Broadway production of "Jesus Christ Superstar."

Inside Broadway Tours:
www.insidebroadway tours.com

Times Square was still as a meadow at evening, with the sun streaming in on the people.

—George Selden

{ Times Tower }

Planted on West 42nd Street and Broadway, 1 Times Square is the most-coveted advertising locale in the world, where companies pay millions to display electronic billboards on the 25-story facade.

Inside is mainly vacant, but that wasn't always the case. The New York Times erected the tower in 1904 as its headquarters. The neighborhood's name changed from Longacre Square to Times Square in the newspaper's honor. On December 31, 1903, fireworks exploded from the roof to promote the opening and welcome the new year, changing to the lowering of a lit ball a few years later. The paper moved in 1913, but the tradition remains.

In New York's Times Square a white-clad girl clutches her purse and skirt as an uninhibited sailor plants his lips squarely on hers.

—Alfred Eisenstaedt

Where were you when you heard The Beatles sing for the first time on The Ed Sullivan Show?

—Baby Boomers

{ The Ed Sullivan Theater }

The 13-story brick building on the stretch of Broadway between West 53rd and West 54th streets didn't always bear Ed Sullivan's name. Arthur Hammerstein opened his venue for musicals in 1927, naming it Hammerstein's Theater after his grandfather, Oscar Hammerstein I. The venue's first show, "The Golden Dawn," featured then-unknown actor Archie Leach—you know him best as leading man Cary Grant.

The venue closed during the Great Depression and reopened later as a dance hall. In 1935, CBS moved in and has been there ever since. In the early days, the network broadcast radio shows, later transforming the theater into a television

The Beatles on "The Ed Sullivan Show," February 9, 1964

studio, where classics like "The Honeymooners," "The Merv Griffin Show," "$10,000 Pyramid" and "Kate & Allie" were filmed.

Of course, the most notable program produced in the space was Ed Sullivan's variety show, which he moved from the Maxine Elliott Theater in 1953 and retooled from "Toast of the Town" to "The Ed Sullivan Show." During its nearly 23-year run, American audiences were introduced to The Beatles, Elvis Presley, The Doors (famously asked never to return after refusing to censor certain lyrics) and many more acts. The theater was renamed after the legendary host on the show's 20th anniversary in 1967.

The Beatles' Ed Sullivan Show Appearance

By the time The Beatles crossed the pond for their first U.S. tour in February 1964, the twentysomething lads from Liverpool, England, were already household names across America. "I Want to Hold Your Hand" had reached No. 1 on the Billboard charts, and kids throughout the country wore Beatle wigs and plastered their cars with "The Beatles Are Coming" bumper stickers in anticipation of "The Ed Sullivan Show" appearance.

The TV host first heard of the band in 1963 while at London's Heathrow Airport, seeing throngs of screeching fans waiting in the rain for The Beatles' return home from Sweden. Later, Sullivan secured a deal for three shows with the band's manager over dinner at Hotel Delmonico.

Over 50,000 people called CBS to secure tickets for the February 9 performance, but the studio could only hold 700 fans. Walter Cronkite, Jack Paar and Richard Nixon got seats for their kids, but even Sullivan had a hard time getting extra tickets, pleading with his audience a week before for spares.

Seventy-three million people tuned in to the first performance. That performance, combined with the subsequent two in 1964 and a return appearance the next year, attracted a quarter of a billion viewers.

Seventy-three million people watched "The Ed Sullivan Show" on February 9, 1964

Everywhere in the world, music enhances a hall, with one exception: Carnegie Hall enhances the music.

—Isaac Stern

{ Carnegie Hall }

Andrew Carnegie funded construction of many venerable NYC buildings, including the Midtown music hall that bears his name. Designed by architect and amateur cellist William Burnet Tuthill in the Renaissance Revival style, the fortress-like structure (made almost entirely of stone and masonry) opened to much fanfare with a five-day celebration on May 5, 1891.

The opening-night concert included Pyotr Ilich Tchaikovsky's Marche Solennelle. Since then, more than 46,000 events have taken place in the landmark's three auditoriums.

The hall was built to house the Oratorio Society of New York and New York Symphony Society. Later, the New York Philharmonic was the longtime resident orchestra before moving to Lincoln Center.

*Louis Armstrong
at Carnegie Hall,
William P. Gottlieb,
1947*

Not just a space for classical music, The Beatles played the historic venue during their first U.S. tour, paving the way for other rock acts like the Rolling Stones, Ike & Tina Turner and Led Zeppelin. Given the sharp acoustics, the interior is also a good space for lectures. Famous orators who have spoken there include Booker T. Washington, Mark Twain and Winston Churchill.

Called "Music Hall founded by Andrew Carnegie" when it opened, the name was later shortened to Carnegie Hall. You can still see the original sign above the marquee.

Andrew Carnegie's Contribution to New York

Andrew Carnegie, c. 1913

In 1889, Andrew Carnegie, a steel magnate and one of the richest men of the 19th century, published "The Gospel of Wealth." In it, he argued that wealthy citizens had a moral obligation to use their riches to help society's advancement.

A few years later, he used his sizable bank account to fund construction of the Midtown music hall that now bears his name. By 1901, he switched his focus from business to philanthropic work, selling his steel empire, Carnegie Steel Corporation, to J.P. Morgan's United States Steel Corporation. He used the $480 million paycheck, along with his considerable earnings over the years, to devote the rest of his life to charitable endeavors throughout the world.

From his mansion on the Upper East Side (now the Cooper Hewitt, Smithsonian Design Museum), his wealth funded several New York projects. A self-educated man and avid reader, Carnegie believed everyone should have access to books. His millions helped open branches of the New York Public Library throughout the city. One of the last organizations he founded before his death was the Carnegie Corporation of New York. Now more than 100 years old, the corporation still promotes education and world peace.

Upper East Side

The city seen from the Queensboro Bridge is always the city seen for the first time, in its first wild promise of all the mystery and beauty in the world.

—F. Scott Fitzgerald

{ Ed Koch Queensboro Bridge }

Spanning 7,449 feet, this historic overpass is the longest of the four major East River bridges and the only one that's not a suspension model. Built between 1901 and 1909 to connect Midtown Manhattan to Long Island City in Queens, thousands of motorists and pedestrians use the cantilever crossing daily.

Nicknamed the 59th Street Bridge, each year runners and cyclists traverse its paths during the New York City Marathon and Five Boro Bike Tour. Although not as famous as its counterparts to the south, it's been featured in screwball comedies like "My Man Godfrey" and love stories like Woody Allen's "Manhattan."

*We immediately set about obtaining
a comfortable lodging-house in the
neighbourhood of the city, and at length
pitched our tent at Mount Vernon, about
four miles from New York, on the East
River or Long Island Sound, a good house
in an airy situation, from the door of
which a stage went to New York two or
three times a-day.*

—James Stuart, a Scottish diarist

{ Mount Vernon Hotel Museum & Garden }

This Georgian-style, Upper East Side gem was built
in 1799 as the carriage house for Colonel William
Stephens Smith and wife Abigail Adams Smith's
23-acre estate. The home burned down in 1826, and
the building was converted into a country day resort.

Located just a few yards from the East River, the
hotel (far north of the city at that time) was where
wealthy New Yorkers would rest after spending the
day sunbathing near the river, wading in its waters
and eating oysters.

The hotel closed in 1833, and the building was
reopened as a museum (restored to its former glory)
in 1939.

*If anybody starts using me as scenery,
I'll return to New York.*

—Grace Kelly

{ Barbizon Hotel for Women }

From 1927 to 1981, female New Yorkers found a safe place to call home at The Barbizon Hotel for Women. Although rooms were small and bathrooms were shared, the Upper East Side hotel did include an indoor pool. Joan Crawford, Grace Kelly and Rita Hayworth were notable tenants. Writer Sylvia Plath also lived here, a fictionalized version of the hotel (The Amazon) features in her semiautobiographical novel "The Bell Jar."

Male guests were admitted in 1981, and the property operated as The Melrose Hotel from 2002 to 2005. Today, the 140 East 63rd Street address is Barbizon 63, a condominium complex.

The Park Avenue of poodles and polished brass; it is cab country, tip-town, glassville, a window-washer's paradise.

—Gay Talese

{ 740 Park Avenue }

The city's most expensive apartment building rests at 740 Park Avenue on the Upper East Side. The limestone-clad structure is one of the toughest places to get an apartment (the co-op board has turned down Barbara Walters and Barbra Streisand).

An uptown fixture since 1929, the structure was designed by architects Rosario Candela and Arthur Loomis Harmon. Jacqueline Kennedy Onassis grew up here; her grandfather, James T. Lee, built the 31-unit property. The crème de la crème is the 24-room, 12-bath "Rockefeller" apartment, where John D. Rockefeller Jr. lived from 1937 to 1960. Since then, it has been sold for upward of $30 million.

*But if I had to choose a single
destination where I'd be held captive
for the rest of my time in New York, I'd
choose the Metropolitan Museum of Art.*

—Tim Gunn

{ The Metropolitan Museum of Art }

At a dinner party in Paris on July 4, 1866, John Jay, president of the Union League Club of New York, presented a crowd of American businessmen and politicians with an idea, the founding of a national institution and art gallery.

The Metropolitan Museum of Art opened in 1872 at 681 Fifth Avenue in Midtown and counted a Roman sarcophagus and 174 European paintings as some of its first holdings. Today, the sprawling institution boasts more than two million works from around the world, including a comprehensive collection of antiquities; Egyptian art; arms and armor; European paintings and more.

The Met moved to its current site on March 30, 1880, settling into a Calvert Vaux and Jacob Wrey Mould-designed, Victorian Gothic-style, redbrick building across from Central Park. With additions by several architects in subsequent years, namely Richard Morris Hunt, little remains of the museum's original structure.

But if you want a peek at The Met's past, you just need to know where to look. Two of the building's original staircases can be seen in the European Paintings and Medieval Art galleries while a banded-granite pointed arch, part of the 1880 facade, sits at the top of the Robert Wood Johnson Jr. Gallery.

*The Mall in Central Park near the
Metropolitan Museum, 1902*

No man is a true gentleman who does not inspire the affection and devotion of his servants.

—Andrew Carnegie

{ Andrew Carnegie's Mansion }

In 1898, steel industry magnate Andrew Carnegie wanted a wide-open space to build a modest, yet roomy, residence in which to raise his daughter. He selected 91st Street and Fifth Avenue, far from mansions farther south, and employed Babb, Cook & Willard for the job. The roomy, although opulent, house was completed in 1901—a Georgian-style marvel with 64 rooms, beautiful wood moldings throughout, private Otis elevator, central heat, precursor to AC and expansive garden.

After retiring, Carnegie conducted philanthropic work here. His widow stayed until her death in 1946. Since 1976, it has housed the Cooper Hewitt, Smithsonian Design Museum.

I wake up every morning and say to myself, 'Well, I'm still in New York. Thank you, God.'
—Ed Koch

{ Gracie Mansion }

In 1799, merchant Archibald Gracie built a wooden, Federal-style country house five miles north of the city (now the Upper East Side), overlooking the East River. In 1896, city officials used the 11-acre grounds for Carl Schurz Park.

Housing concessions for the public park and later the Museum of the City of New York, the mansion became the mayor of New York's official residence in 1942 when Fiorello H. La Guardia moved in.

Only family and official guests are allowed to stay overnight, making it an unsuitable home for bachelor mayors. Tours are available.

There has never been a problem with the 100-foot buffer.
—James Renwick Jr.

{ Renwick Smallpox Hospital }

The influx of immigrants in the mid-1800s meant the city was plagued with smallpox. Designed by architect James Renwick Jr. in a neo-Gothic style, the hospital opened on Blackwell's (now Roosevelt) Island in 1856. By 1875, it had become a training center for nurses. Abandoned today, it is nevertheless open to visitors and is the city's only ruin with National Landmark status.

The insane asylum on Blackwell's Island is a human rat-trap. It is easy to get in, but once there it is impossible to get out. —Nellie Bly

{ The Insane of Blackwell's Island }

Roosevelt Island, then Blackwell's Island, housed an insane asylum built in 1834. Charles Dickens once visited the asylum, describing its painful "madhouse air" in his "American Notes." Journalist Nellie Bly stayed there undercover and reported on the deplorable conditions. Closed in 1894, all that remains is The Octagon (main entrance). You can climb the staircase.

Upper West Side

HUDSON RIVER

HENRY HUDSON PARKWAY

RIVERSIDE DRIVE

BROADWAY

82ND STREET

79TH STREET

AMERICAN MUSEUM OF
NATURAL HISTORY

92

AMSTERDAM AVENUE

COLUMBUS AVENUE

89

91

72ND STREET

90

WEST END AVENUE

CENTRAL PARK WEST

LINCOLN CENTER FOR
THE PERFORMING ARTS

65TH STREET

88

CENTRAL PARK

87

TENTH AVENUE

COLUMBUS CIRCLE

EIGHTH AVENUE

59TH STREET

But you do have to learn, if you want to be a satirist, you can't be part of the party. Meaning, you can't go horseback riding with Jackie O in Central Park if you're going to make a joke about her that night.

—Joan Rivers

{ Central Park }

In the 1850s, wealthy citizens wanted to build a magnificent public park to rival the green spaces of London and Paris and place New York on the map as a cosmopolitan destination.

Not quite central at the time, land was picked on the city's northern reaches to build the nation's first landscaped public park. Although the 700-acre-plus area was full of swamps, bluffs and rock formations, it was by no means a wilderness. More than 1,600 people lived there, including Irish and German immigrants and middle-class African Americans, who lived in flourishing Seneca Village. All were kicked out due to "eminent domain."

Central Park, c. 1900

Frederick Law Olmsted and Calvert Vaux designed the grassy grounds—a mix of manicured lawns, bridges, pathways, the Bethesda Terrace and fountain, and more than 270,000 trees and shrubs. Since its 1858 opening, the park has been a peaceful sojourn from the surrounding city. Heavily renovated over the years, some of the park's earliest vegetation still exists, including the Yoshino cherry trees on the east side of the Reservoir, given to the U.S. by Japan in 1912. All that remains of Seneca Village is a foundation near 85th Street.

Millions of people enjoy the park—now grown to 843 acres—each year.

Frederick Law Olmsted and New York

Frederick Law Olmsted, 1893

Connecticut native Frederick Law Olmsted intended to go to Yale University, but sumac poisoning weakened his eyesight and derailed his college plans. In 1848, he settled on a 125-acre farm in Staten Island and became a prominent newspaper man—writing about public gardens in England and later working as a traveling correspondent for the New York Daily Times (now The New York Times), covering the social and economic repercussions of slavery in the American South. He also worked for Putman's Magazine and The Nation.

Olmsted had a successful journalism career, but he is more widely known as the father of landscape architecture. Ironically, when tapped to design Central Park, he knew little about the subject. He met Calvert Vaux through The Horticulturist magazine's publisher, Andrew Jackson Downing. Vaux, impressed with Olmsted's beliefs and contacts, offered him the opportunity of a lifetime, the chance to be his partner in the design competition for Central Park. The duo won, and their partnership resulted in Manhattan's most famous green space, as well as Prospect Park in Brooklyn. Through his own company, Olmsted designed Queens' Forest Park and several other city projects. He was also a founding member of the prestigious Union League Club of New York.

I fell in love with New York. It was like every human being, like any relationship. When I was a young New Yorker, it was one city. When I was a grown man, it was another city.

—Mikhail Baryshnikov

{ Lincoln Center for the Performing Arts }

The 16.3-acre plot occupied by Lincoln Center was formerly San Juan Hill, a densely populated African-American and Puerto Rican section of low-rise tenements and street gangs.

As part of an urban renewal project, the neighborhood was leveled, forcing 40,000 people to relocate. President Eisenhower broke ground in 1959, and President Kennedy attended the inaugural performance at Philharmonic Hall (the center's first venue) in 1962. The New York Philharmonic, Metropolitan Opera and New York City Ballet perform in the complex's various buildings. You can see San Juan Hill in "West Side Story," which was filmed on location.

I look out the window and I see the lights and the skyline and the people on the street rushing around looking for action, love, and the world's greatest chocolate chip cookie, and my heart does a little dance.

—Nora Ephron

{ The Ansonia }

In 1899, Phelps-Dodge copper heir William Earle Dodge Stokes commissioned sculptor Paul E. Duboy to draft plans for a self-sufficient, luxe residential hotel at 2109 Broadway. The well-appointed apartments boasted high ceilings, parlors, libraries and balconies. Building amenities included a rooftop farm, ballroom, Turkish baths, restaurants and a fountain filled with live seals. Jack Dempsey, Babe Ruth and Arnold Rothstein were residents.

Lodgings were subdivided in the mid-1900s. In the 1960s and 1970s, a gay bathhouse operated in the basement, where then-unknown Bette Midler belted out tunes, with Barry Manilow tickling the ivories. The Upper West Side's Beaux Arts-style gem now houses luxury condos.

If I'd lived in Roman times, I'd have lived in Rome. Where else? Today America is the Roman Empire and New York is Rome itself.

—John Lennon

{ The Dakota Apartments }

When the Gothic-style Dakota apartment building was constructed in 1884, it was located so far northwest of the city that its remote location led some to muse "it might as well have been built in the Dakotas." When completed, the Edward Clark-designed marvel was a groundbreaking advancement in modern city living, offering electricity, indoor plumbing, elevators and room service.

During its 130-year-plus reign on the Upper West Side, a "who's who" of celebrities have called the structure home, including Boris Karloff, Lauren Bacall and Judy Garland. John Lennon lived here with Yoko Ono from 1973 until his murder outside

John Lennon and Yoko Ono at Madison Square Garden in 1972

the building in 1980. Ono is said to have felt the ghost of her late husband inside their home. Other ghosts that walk the halls include a little boy and a girl with long blond hair. In the basement, an apparition of a short man with a beard, wire-framed glasses and top hat has been known to throw items throughout the space. The description matches Edward Clark.

Although you can't go inside to see Lennon's ghost, you can honor the legendary Beatle in Central Park. Directly across from The Dakota, the Strawberry Fields mosaic is a tribute to the slain musician.

Give me such shows—give me the streets of Manhattan!

—*Walt Whitman*

{ New-York Historical Society Museum & Library }

Founded in 1804, the New-York Historical Society is the city's oldest museum. From its Upper West Side home—a York & Sawyer-designed, Roman Eclectic-style building dating back to 1908—the institution presents history and art exhibitions that explore the ever-changing political, social and cultural climate of NYC, the state and the country. The facility also boasts a comprehensive research library.

The American Museum of Natural History is my son's absolute favorite place in the world! So we really, really, really love New York.

—*Mark Teixeira*

{ American Museum of Natural History }

The American Museum of Natural History began life in the early 1870s as a cabinet of curiosities located in the Central Park Arsenal.

When the museum grew too big for its space, a larger facility was erected across the street from the park. President Ulysses S. Grant laid the cornerstone for the museum's first building in 1874, a Calvert Vaux and Jacob Wrey Mould-designed, Victorian Gothic structure. The museum opened in 1877 but, unfortunately, just because you build it, doesn't mean people will come. With few visitors, museum president Morris K. Jesup decided to change the game plan, sponsoring

global expeditions (explorations that discovered the North Pole, dinosaur fossils in Mongolia and more) and bringing the findings back home for display.

Today, more than 32 million specimens and artifacts are presented in permanent exhibition halls throughout 28 interconnecting buildings—Richardsonian Romanesque and Beaux Arts-style expansions to the museum's original home.

Visitors can check out lifelike dioramas; Lucy, a 3.18-million-year-old hominid skeleton (she got her name from The Beatles' song "Lucy in the Sky With Diamonds"); and a 94-foot-long model of a blue whale. They can also stargaze in the planetarium. The first-floor Hall of Northwest Coast Indians is part of the original building.

Miss Elizabeth Haldane (wearing hat with white plume), sister of Viscount Haldane; Judge Dickinson (carrying umbrella), and J.P. Morgan at the Columbia Yacht Club, located at the foot of 86th Street and the Hudson River, 1913

Harlem and North

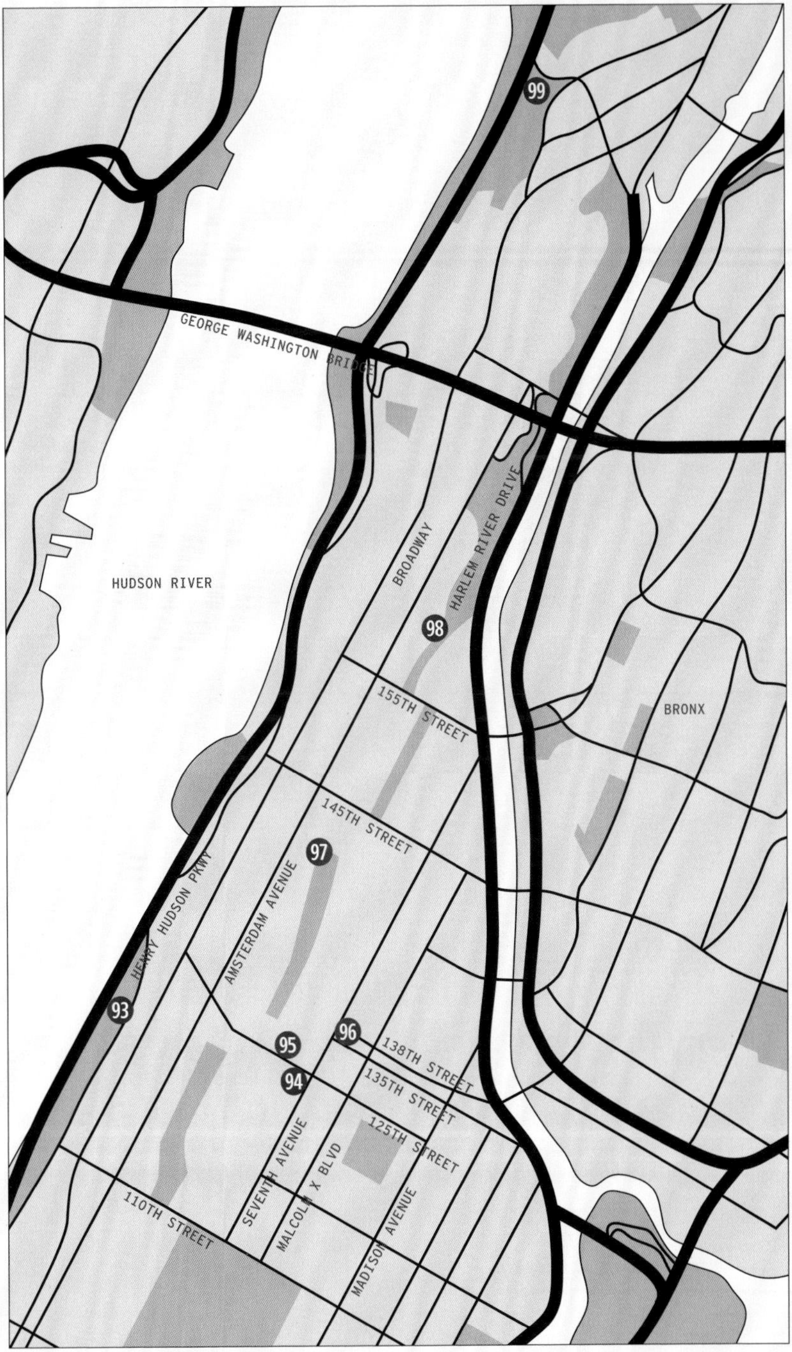
GEORGE WASHINGTON BRIDGE
HUDSON RIVER
BROADWAY
HARLEM RIVER DRIVE
155TH STREET
BRONX
145TH STREET
AMSTERDAM AVENUE
HENRY HUDSON PKWY
138TH STREET
135TH STREET
125TH STREET
SEVENTH AVENUE
MALCOLM X BLVD
MADISON AVENUE
110TH STREET
93
94
95
96
97
98
99

Riverside was selected by myself and my family as the burial place of my husband, General Grant. First, because I believed New York was his preference.

—Julia Grant

{ General Grant National Memorial }

Although President Ulysses S. Grant commanded Northern troops during the Civil War, Confederate and Union generals attended his funeral on August 8, 1885. Over one million mourners, including President Grover Cleveland, marched in the seven-mile-long funeral parade through New York City.

Grant's body rested in a temporary tomb in Riverside Park while funds were raised to build the John Duncan-designed mausoleum, the largest in North America. He was placed there in 1897, and his wife, Julia, joined him in 1902. Run by the National Parks Service, the monument fell into disrepair in the 1980s but was restored the following decade.

My favorite thing about New York is the people, because I think they're misunderstood. I don't think people realize how kind New York people are.

—Bill Murray

{ Hotel Theresa }

Known as "The Waldorf of Harlem," Hotel Theresa was the site of many historic events. Opened in 1913 as whites-only lodgings, the terra-cotta-clad structure had an African-American staff and multiethnic clientele by 1940. Fidel Castro and his entourage famously checked in after storming out of Midtown's Shelburne Hotel, accused of causing $10,000 worth of damages. His visitors included Nikita Khrushchev and Malcom X. The latter later used the building for his Organization of Afro-American Unity headquarters. It was also a stop on John F. Kennedy's presidential campaign tour. The hotel was converted into an office building, Theresa Towers, in 1970.

New York is a place where the rich walk, the poor drive Cadillacs, and beggars die of malnutrition with thousands of dollars hidden in their mattresses.

—*Duke Ellington*

{ Apollo Theater }

With a red neon sign visible up and down 125th Street, the Apollo Theater is one of Harlem's most recognizable attractions.

Opened in 1914, the George Keister-designed, neoclassical structure began life as Hurtig and Seamon's New Burlesque Theater, off limits to African-American patrons and performers. The venue closed in 1933 and reopened under new management the following year, catering to Harlem's growing African-American community. On opening night, the diverse lineup included black jazz musician Benny Carter, white comic Ralph Cooper and black singer Aida Ward. Dancer Bill "Bojangles"

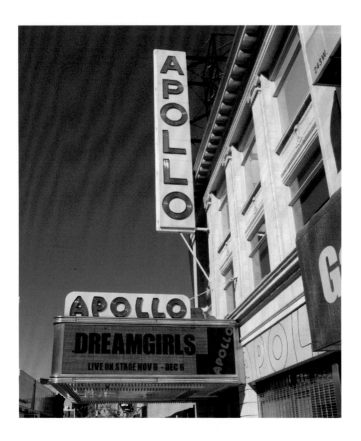

Robinson and comedian Nipsey Russell were also popular early acts.

Not just open to established stars, the venue also welcomes new talent during Amateur Night competitions, letting audiences determine the next big names in entertainment. Past winners have included Ella Fitzgerald, Pearl Bailey, Gladys Knight and Jimi Hendrix.

A young James Brown was an Amateur Night contestant in the 1950s, returning as a headliner the following decade. When the Godfather of Soul died in 2006, his body lay in state on the Apollo stage for thousands of mourners to pay their respects. When Michael Jackson died in 2009, music fans again congregated in the venerable venue to honor the King of Pop.

Billie Holiday's Life in New York

Billie Holiday led a life full of ups and downs, most of which happened during her time in New York City.

Born in Philadephia in 1915 as Eleanora Fagan, Holiday moved to Harlem when she was 13 years old to live with her mother. She took up her mother's trade, working as a prostitute in a neighborhood brothel. Later, she began singing in local clubs under the stage name Billie Holiday. She made her debut at the Apollo Theater when she was 19 and would go on to appear there nearly 30 times during her career.

While making the rounds in jazz clubs, she met talent scout John Hammond. He was able to get her recording work with Benny Goodman and Teddy Wilson and later tours with Count Basie and Artie Shaw's orchestras.

Billie Holiday at the Apollo Theater, 1944

Holiday honed her public persona on the stage of Greenwich Village's Café Society, donning gardenias in her hair and debuting "Strange Fruit," one of her biggest hits. In 1948, she performed a sold-out show at Carnegie Hall.

A longtime drug addict and alcoholic, Holiday's demons caught up with her in 1959. That July, she died in East Harlem's Metropolitan Hospital due to complications from drug and alcohol abuse.

I want to establish the kingdom of social justice.

—*Adam Clayton Powell Sr.*

{ Abyssinian Baptist Church }

In 1808, visiting Ethiopian seamen attended services at the First Baptist Church in the City of New York. When segregated from white churchgoers, they, along with African Americans, left in protest, fueling the founding of Abyssinian Baptist Church.

After occupying several locations, pastor Adam Clayton Powell Sr. secured a permanent home for the church in the 1920s in newly formed Harlem. During his son's tenure (1937 to 1971), membership reached over 10,000—the largest Protestant congregation in the nation. Nat King Cole was married in the Gothic- and Tudor-style church in 1948. Today, you can attend services and hear the celebrated gospel choir.

A garden, you know, is a very usual
refuge of a disappointed politician.

—Alexander Hamilton

{ Hamilton Grange }

Revolutionary War hero, U.S. secretary of treasury and ill-fated loser in a duel with Aaron Burr, Alexander Hamilton has received a lot of love as of late. Armchair historians, avid theatergoers and everyone in between are flocking to see the imaginative retelling of his life (in hip-hop form) in the aptly named Broadway hit "Hamilton."

If you want to learn more about the man while waiting for those hard-to-get tickets, just take a quick trip uptown to Hamilton Grange, the Founding Father's last home.

The John McComb Jr.-designed, Federal-style country house was built on Hamilton's 32-acre estate in secluded

View across the upper Harlem valley, looking to the north, 1762–1780

upper Manhattan (now Harlem) in 1802, where he lived until his death in 1804.

St. Luke's Episcopal Church bought the house in 1889 and moved it a few blocks south to 287 Convent Avenue, dismantling several features to make transport easier. It sat at the address for more than 100 years, first used for church services and later as a museum, while Harlem quickly developed around it.

The historic structure was designated a National Memorial in the 1960s and was moved again in 2009, this time to St. Nicholas Park. Carefully restored, the two-story house once again resembles its original design. Guided tours are available.

Hamilton's Life in New York

Born in the West Indies, Alexander Hamilton heard about Britain's conflicts with American colonists and wanted to prove himself in battle. He moved to New York in 1774 to attend King's College (now Columbia University) and, a year later, finally got his chance.

With the Revolutionary War suspending his education, Hamilton eagerly joined the New York State provincial militia. He met General George Washington, moved up the ranks and became one of Washington's most-trusted soldiers.

After the revolution, Hamilton began his career as a New York attorney, taking up residence with his family at 57 Wall Street and fighting for Tories to regain their properties seized during the war. He helped establish the Bank of New York and was later named Secretary of the Treasury under President Washington.

Hamilton's political opinions earned him many enemies, and one of his biggest foes was Vice President Aaron Burr. In 1804, Hamilton articulated his disdain for the man in a published letter. The insult fueled a heated argument, which culminated in a duel on July 11 in Weehawken, New Jersey. Hamilton was wounded and died the following day. He is buried in Trinity Church cemetery, and you can visit his last home in Harlem.

Alexander Hamilton, John Trumbull, 1806

I give you my hand, Madame (Eliza); my heart has long been yours.

—*Aaron Burr*

{ Morris–Jumel Mansion }

In 1765, British Colonel Roger Morris built a summer villa on a 130-acre plot on the banks of the Harlem River in today's Washington Heights. It is the oldest remaining house in Manhattan.

General George Washington used the Palladian-style estate as his headquarters. As president, he dined with John Adams, Thomas Jefferson and John Quincy Adams there. In 1810, merchant Stephen Jumel and his wife, Eliza, bought the home. When widowed, Eliza would go on to marry Aaron Burr in the house. They divorced, but she stayed until her death in 1865. Transformed into a museum in 1904, Eliza's ghost haunts the halls.

Think of giving not as a duty but as a privilege.

—John D. Rockefeller Jr.

{ The Met Cloisters }

The Cloisters, nestled in Fort Tryon Park in Manhattan's bucolic northern reaches, resembles a monastery and houses The Metropolitan Museum of Art's medieval European art collection. Comprised of reassembled pieces from five medieval French cloisters (Saint-Michel-de-Cuxa, Saint-Guilhem-le-Désert, Bonnefont-en-Comminges, Trie-en-Bigorre and Froville), as well as Gothic- and Romanesque-style chapels, the complex rests on four acres, overlooks the Hudson River and includes aromatic gardens.

John D. Rockefeller Jr. funded construction of the museum, which opened in 1938, as well as the adjacent park. Today, the collection includes more than 2,000 artworks and architectural pieces. The park holds a Medieval Festival in early fall.

Historic Landmarks of Old New York

The Statue of Liberty (page 10)
Liberty Island, NY 10004
www.nps.gov/stli/index.htm

Ellis Island (page 14)
Ellis Island Museum of Immigration,
NY 10004, www.nps.gov/elis/index.htm

Castle Clinton (page 16)
Battery Park, NY 10004
www.nps.gov/cacl/index.htm

Fraunces Tavern (page 18)
54 Pearl St, NY 10004
frauncestavernmuseum.org

Stone Street Historic District (page 22)
Stone St, NY 10004
www.nycgo.com/articles/must-see-
financial-district-slideshow

India House (page 24)
1 Hanover Square, NY 10004
www.indiahouseclub.org

20 Exchange Place (page 26)
20 Exchange Pl, NY 10005
www.20xnyc.com

55 Wall Street–Merchant Exchange
(page 28), 55 Wall St, NY 10005
www.cipriani.com

Federal Reserve Building (page 29)
33 Liberty St, NY 10045
www.newyorkfed.org

Federal Hall (page 30)
26 Wall St, NY 10005
www.nps.gov/feha/index.htm

New York Stock Exchange (page 34)
11 Wall St, NY 10005
www.nyse.com

Trinity Church (page 36)
75 Broadway, NY 10006
www.trinitywallstreet.org

St. Paul's Chapel (page 40)
209 Broadway, NY 10007, www.trinity
wallstreet.org/about/stpaulschapel

The Woolworth Building (page 44)
233 Broadway, NY 10007
thewoolworthtower.com

Brooklyn Bridge (page 46)
Brooklyn Bridge, NY 10038
www.nyc.gov/html/dot/html/infrastruc
ture/brooklyn-bridge.shtml

New York City Hall (page 50)
City Hall Park, NY 10007
www.nycgo.com/attractions/city-hall

African Burial Ground (page 54)
290 Broadway, NY 10007
www.nps.gov/afbg/index.htm

Eldridge Street Synagogue (page 58)
12 Eldridge St, NY 10002
www.eldridgestreet.org

Tenement Museum (page 60)
103 Orchard St, NY 10002
www.tenement.org

The Police Building (page 64)
240 Centre St, NY 10013

The Ear Inn (page 66)
326 Spring St, NY 10013
www.earinn.com

St. Luke's Place (page 68)
St Lukes Pl, NY 10014

Judson Memorial Church (page 70)
55 Washington Square S, NY 10012
www.judson.org

Washington Square Park (page 72)
Washington Square Park, NY 10012
washingtonsquareparkconservancy.org

MacDougal Alley (page 76)
MacDougal Alley, NY 10011

Washington Mews (page 77)
Washington Mews, NY 10003

Jefferson Market Courthouse (page 80)
425 Sixth Ave, NY 10011, www.nypl.org/
about/locations/jefferson-market

Stonewall Inn (page 82)
53 Christopher St, NY 10014
www.thestonewallinnnyc.com

Marie's Crisis Cafe (page 86)
59 Grove St, NY 10014

Cherry Lane Theatre (page 88)
38 Commerce St, NY 10014
www.cherrylanetheatre.org

102 Bedford Street (page 90)
102 Bedford St, NY 10014

The Church of St. Luke in the Fields
(page 91), 487 Hudson St, NY 10014
www.stlukeinthefields.org

69 Charles Street (page 92)
69 Charles St, NY 10014

White Horse Tavern (page 94)
567 Hudson St, NY 10014
www.whitehorsetavern1880.com

Westbeth–Bell Laboratories Building
(page 96), 55 Bethune St, NY 10014
www.westbeth.org

Grace Church (page 100)
802 Broadway, NY 10003
gracechurchnyc.org

The Cooper Union Foundation Building
(page 104), 7 East 7th St, NY 10003
cooper.edu

Astor Library (page 106)
425 Lafayette St, NY 10003
www.publictheater.org

Colonnade Row (page 108)
428, 430, 432 and 434 Lafayette St,
NY 10003

Merchant's House (page 109)
29 E 4th St, NY 10003
merchantshouse.org

McSorley's Old Ale House (page 110)
15 E 7th St, NY 10003
mcsorleysoldalehouse.nyc

St. Mark's Church in-the-Bowery
(page 114), 131 East 10th St, NY 10003
stmarksbowery.org

Union Square (page 118)
Union Square, NY 10003
unionsquarenyc.org

Pete's Tavern (page 121)
129 East 18th St, NY 10003
www.petestavern.com

1972, (Bettmann/Getty Images); **Page 244:** American Museum of Natural History, Detroit Publishing Co., c. 1902, Library of Congress, LC-D4-14285; **Page 247:** Miss Elizabeth Haldane (wearing hat with white plume), sister of Viscount Haldane; Judge Dickinson (carrying umbrella), and J.P. Morgan at the Columbia Yacht Club, located at the foot of 86th Street, Bain News Service, 1913, Library of Congress, LC-B2- 2808-3; **Page 250:** Riverside Park, Detroit Publishing Co., between 1900 and 1906, Library of Congress, LC-D418-13391; **Page 252:** Apollo Theatre, Hotel Theresa and Blumstein Dept. Store on 125th Street in Harlem. (Photo by Budd Williams/NY Daily News Archive via Getty Images); **Page 254:** Performers during their act on amateur night in front of large crowd at the Apollo Theater on 125th St. in Harlem. (Photo by Herbert Gehr/The LIFE Picture Collection/Getty Images); **Page 258:** Exterior view of the Abyssinian Baptist Church, c. 1923. (Photo by George Rinhart/Corbis via Getty Images); **Page 265:** Jumel Mansion, Detroit Publishing Co., c. 1904, Library of Congress, LC-D4-17538; **Page 272:** Night scene in Manhattan, Berenice Abbott, 1976, Library of Congress, LC-DIG-ds-00188; **Page 23, 24, 30, 37, 40, 46, 54, 58, 61, 64, 68, 71, 74, 77, 82, 86, 88, 90, 96, 100, 106, 109, 112, 118, 121, 122, 128, 129, 130, 142, 146, 148, 156, 160, 168, 172, 180, 183, 190, 196, 202, 207, 212, 219, 220, 232, 236, 243, 256, 260, 267** Photos by Alex Child

Double your enjoyment by reading "Chronicles of Old New York" by James Roman!, a companion volume chock-full of useful maps, neighborhood walking tours and detailed stories about the landmarks.

Chronicles of Old New York
by James Roman
ISBN 978-1-940842-08-0
Trade Paperback (full color)
308 pages, 5 1/4" x 8"
$19.95

CONTRIBUTING WRITER

Mackenzie Allison

Mackenzie Grace Allison is a New York City-based writer and editor. She has made a career writing about travel and tourism, both in the United States and abroad. Through her writing, she is thrilled to give NYC locals, visitors and everyone in between an up-close look at this dynamic metropolis.

ABOUT MUSEYON

Named after the Mouseion, the ancient library of Alexandria, Museyon is a New York City-based independent publisher that explores cultural obsessions such as art, history and travel. Expertly curated and carefully researched, Museyon books offer rich entertainment, with fascinating anecdotes, beautiful images and quality information.

Publisher: Akira Chiba
Editor: Francis Lewis
Image Editor: Emi Robinson
Cover Designer: José Antonio Contreras